WHAT ENGLISH TEACHERS WANT

A Survival Guide

by
Susan Vreeland

Second Printing

Royal Fireworks Press
Unionville, New York
Toronto, Ontario

TO MY STUDENTS,
OF THE SAN DIEGO UNIFIED SCHOOL DISTRICT,
WHO NEVER CEASE
TO TEACH ME LESSONS

Special thanks to Cory Garfin whose careful editing gave me the students' perspective, and so much more.

Royal Fireworks Press
First Avenue
Unionville, NY 10988
(914) 726-4444
FAX: (914) 726-3824

Royal Fireworks Press
78 Biddeford Avenue
Downsview, Ontario
M3H 1K4 Canada
FAX: (416) 633-3010

ISBN: 0-88092-224-9 Paperback

Printed in the United States of America using soy-based inks on acid-free, recycled paper by the Royal Fireworks Press of Unionville, New York.

TABLE OF CONTENTS

iii

FOREWORD

Take heart. If you panic at the thought of having to write an essay, this handbook is for you.

If you don't know when to use "good" and when to use "well," and you don't know how to look it up, this handbook is also for you. Perhaps your essays are returned dripping with red ink. You'd like to know how to avoid writing sentence fragments, but you don't know a conjunction from an adjective, so grammar books are intimidating and so you continue to do the best you can just by guessing. This book is for you, too. Maybe your writing is usually clear and you manage to answer the essay questions asked of you, but you still get "C's" and the comment, "Your writing style is awkward," or, worse, "childish," but you don't know how to write as they do in books. Maybe you're afraid of going to college with your writing sounding like you just came in from playing tag. If any of these suspicions have crossed your mind, this handbook has something to offer you.

Few books on writing focus on teaching the most common kind of writing in English classes, the critical essay on a subject from literature. This one does. It also gives a student-written sample, in several drafts, with teacher evaluation. Many books assume you already have a knowledge of terms, and so they're hard to comprehend. Here, terms are explained where they are needed in order to understand a grammar concept.

How to Use This Handbook:

Parts of this book are intended to be read through and studied. Section II, "What is a Critical Essay?" is an example. If you read it each time before you begin writing an essay assignment, your teacher's expectations will be more clear in your mind. Some sections are intended as reference only and should be consulted when you have doubts about some minor point. The use of *good* and *well*, for example, or *lie* and *lay*, *effect* and *affect* are covered in Section XI, "Usage." When you are unsure of punctuation, check the punctuation section. When you receive an assignment back and the graded commentary indicates specific grammar errors, turn to the index to find the appropriate section and compare your mistake to the examples given. After you write a draft for an assignment, examine it in light of Section VII, "How to Revise and Edit." When you don't know how to start and feel frustrated or inadequate, read Section I, "An Encouraging Word," even if you've already read it. It will make you feel better. Everyone can improve his or her own writing. Here are some tools to improve yours. The more you use this handbook, the better your writing is likely to become. It's up to you.

AN ENCOURAGING WORD

No one said writing well was easy. In fact, easy writing is hard reading. First draft writing or informal writing where we just let it roll without concern for style or grammar may be therapeutic, but it rarely sparkles and often fails to meet requirements. In fact, it may be so loose that it is unclear, the worst fault of all communication. To produce final draft writing takes repeated readings to edit out weak or wordy phrases and to uncover grammatical errors.

It's too much to ask yourself to produce a final copy at one sitting; writing that is clear, grammatically correct, stylistically sophisticated, insightful and appropriate to the topic isn't written all at once. If you sign your name to a blank page, assuming that you will submit that very piece of paper, and then you set out to complete an assignment right then, you are placing undue pressure on yourself.

You would do better simply to jot down ideas at they come to you, incomplete as they may be. Let them come freely without regard to form. Just write. Sentences are fine but so are phrases at this point. Even a list of words or subtopics and a few examples will serve to get your thinking started. Each phrase might be worked into a paragraph, but a paragraph won't grow from nothing. Section IV, "Procedures for Writing Essays," gives you ways to start.

At this point of just jotting down thoughts, if you are too concerned about how to say something, or even with how to spell something, that concern flashing across your mind for a fraction of a second might be enough to distract you from your thought and then you may lose it. Instead, when the ideas come, scramble to get them down. Abbreviate. Spell only the first few letters of difficult words. Guess. If you can't think of the right word, draw a line and go on to the rest of your thought, or use a word that comes to mind but isn't quite right. Then, when the rush of ideas dies, go back and work the ideas into correct sentences. After that, look up words in a dictionary for spelling and in a thesaurus for a more appropriate choice.

No one learned to ski by sitting in the snow looking up at a ski slope. Likewise, no one learned to write by staring at an empty page hoping a brilliant opening sentence would spring fully grown onto the page. Write anything just to begin. Then refine. Do you think great authors produced perfect prose every time they formed a sentence? No. They agonized, changed, threw out, changed again. Let's give ourselves the same opportunity.

WHAT IS A CRITICAL ESSAY?

A critical essay is a composition that seeks to analyze and interpret art—in this case, a piece of literature. It does not necessarily criticize the literature negatively. It may examine only one aspect of the piece of literature, for example, a particular theme, character or idea, or several. It may compare one piece of literature to another, or it may ask you to relate the literature to the time period. Several styles of essay questions are explained in Section III, "Common Types of Essay Questions."

Good critical essays present an argument in support of a claim or thesis which is a direct, concise answer to a question posed by the instructor. In fact, the thesis or claim must relate directly to that question and must appear in the opening paragraph in order to serve as an anchor or guide governing the rest of the paper. It is the major point you are going to develop or analyze. All other sentences in your paper must relate to it in some way. If the entire essay could be condensed into one sentence, it would be this thesis sentence, an answer to the essay question, not just a restatement of the question.

Whatever the type of essay question, the answer should not be narrative. That means it should not retell the story in a shortened form. It contains the writer's opinion relative to a particular aspect of a piece of literature, but that is an opinion based closely on the text of the literature itself. In fact, passages from the literary text should be part of the body of your essay.

Most critical essays use a three-part form: introduction, body, and conclusion. In fact, most any kind of expository (non-fiction) writing distinguishes a beginning, a middle, and an end. Many high school instructors prefer a five-paragraph essay, with the body of the paper consisting of three of the five paragraphs. This structure is increasingly seen as too rigid, since many topics don't naturally subdivide into threes. What is generally meant by this instruction is a ratio, that the body generally ought to be at least 3/5 of the length of the whole.

The next page contains a general outline of a critical essay:

I. Introduction   (usually one paragraph)
   A. General comment or observation.   (Not so broad that it's obvious)
   B. Narrowing to specific topic of this paper. (Sometimes A & B are combined into one sentence.)
   C. Title and author of work. (Not a sentence by itself but inserted into a sentence containing other material.)
   D. Background information IF relevant. (time period, setting, social concerns, issue, etc.)
   E. Thesis, the claim of your argument. (see p. 5-6) Usually a one-sentence answer to the question. It should be more than a list of subtopics or a restatement of the question.
   F. Direction of support. Often a list of subtopics or subdivisions of thesis. (The number of subdivisions should be determined by the scope and complexity of question; it's not necessarily always three.)
      1.
      2.
      3.

II. First paragraph of body:
   A. Topic sentence referring to first subdivision. (More than a restatement of subtopic from I. F.)
   B. Analysis, extension, or development of first subtopic. (Discussion in abstract, without reference to specifics of plot; not a quotation.)
   C. Supporting evidence. Could be:
      1. Plot event (not the whole plot of the entire work)
      2. Item related to a character
      3. Reference to imagery, symbolism or allusion
      4. Quotation (with speaker, occasion & interpretation)
      5. Paraphrase (with speaker, occasion & interpretation)
      6. Combination of 1-5
   D. Re-anchor or return to topic sentence and/or thesis
Repeat the same pattern outlined in II for all paragraphs of body

III. Conclusion:

Restatement of thesis only stronger, deeper, more insightful, with reference to subpoints of body

A. Introduction

The introduction is usually a paragraph, sometimes two, rarely one sentence, although that may be enough for a simple topic. The introduction functions to tell the reader what the essay will focus on, what its purpose is. It is a promise of what will follow, and the rest of the essay must deliver on that promise.

Starting Too Far Back:

A common mistake of beginning writers is to start the first sentence so far back from the topic that it sounds empty, obvious or foolish. Examples of this amateurish opening are:

> The Renaissance was an important time period in European history.

> Many writers insert into their work their own ideas or their observations on their time periods.

> *Hamlet* by William Shakespeare contains many forms of writing. In it, there are several soliloquies spoken by Hamlet.

> The concept of satire has been present in our world since the beginning of mankind.

> Throughout the centuries, revenge has changed the course of history.

> Since the dawn of time, the legitimacy of revenge has been a widely disputed issue.

> Nothing is more sincerely touching than tragedy.

None of these give an impression of the writer as an incisive thinker. Please avoid these "dawn of time" openings. Get closer to your subject right from the start.

Somewhere in the introduction, not necessarily the first couple of sentences, the title of the original piece of literature and its author should appear. Imbed this in a sentence that has a more substantial purpose. Giving it a sentence of its own will sound juvenile.

If the essay is to answer a specific question, that question stated as a sentence or issue should be clearly explained, although that explanation is not your thesis. Usually it's best to avoid stating the topic in the form of a question. That's an unimaginative opening. Other unimaginative and inappropriate openings are:

> This essay is about…
> The purpose of this essay is…
> In this essay I'm going to write about…
> I am going to prove that…
> …will be proven.

Don't use any of the these word packages. There's no need to use the word "essay" anywhere in your paper, even in the title. You may begin by setting up the time period in which the narrative takes place, the occasion or premise of a poem, or the social, religious or political attitudes prevalent at the time the work was written, if that is relevant to the essay topic. If the essay topic is actually a series of subtopics, you should start with an umbrella concept that covers or includes them all.

Thesis:

A **thesis or claim of an argument** governs the entire paper and should be consulted frequently as you write the body paragraphs. It sets forth a specific premise in response to the question, and appears in the first paragraph. A good thesis has these characteristics:

1. It makes a substantial, specific claim. It does more than introduce the topic; it answers it.

2. It is precise. It is not something that one has trouble understanding until one reads the rest of the paper, nor is it something so general or so safe that it fails to represent any strong position. For example, "Rigid social practices were important characteristics of the Middle Ages," is not a sufficiently precise statement.

3. It is something worth the argument. It goes beyond arguing a claim so obvious that no one is interested.

4. It is capable of being forcefully supported by the rest of the paper and by reference to the primary text (that is, the novel, poem or play under discussion).

For a lengthy paper, stating the thesis precisely may require more than one sentence, especially if the question involves subtopics. Still, it should stand out from the rest of the opening paragraph as the argument of the paper.

Do not confuse thesis with theme. Simply considered, theme is an author's message in the original piece of literature—or one of several messages. Occasionally, but not always, a theme of the original piece of literature can function as a thesis to your essay, if it answers the question posed by the assignment. Section V deals with how to state a theme.

Here are some questions and appropriate thesis statements:

QUESTION: In what way is *Sir Gawain and the Green Knight* a satire? What is being satirized and what is the tone of his criticism?

THESIS: The author of *Sir Gawain and the Green Knight* uses irony and humor to expose the foolishness of certain customs and attitudes of the Middle Ages, particularly, chivalry, courtly love, and the belief that human perfection is attainable.

Note: Each of these three objects of satire indicated in the thesis should be developed in a separate paragraph. Somewhere in the opening paragraph, it would be good to define satire. Definitions of literary terms are included in the Glossary.

QUESTION: Gertrude Stein said of the 1920's, "We are, after all, a lost generation." How does F. Scott Fitzgerald develop this concept in *The Great Gatsby*?

THESIS: Rather than selflessness or spiritual values, the materialism and search for personal pleasure which Gertrude Stein observed in the 1920's are clearly apparent in F. Scott Fitzgerald's novel, *The Great Gatsby.*

QUESTION: It has been said that *A Farewell to Arms* has a "darkness of perception." Explain what you think this might mean. What is Hemingway's vision of life and love?

THESIS: In *A Farewell to Arms*, Ernest Hemingway demonstrates his dark perception of life by illustrating that in love there is always despair and in life there is ultimately death. Note that in each case, the thesis establishes the use of present tense throughout the essay.

B. Body

The body of the paper contains the development of the ideas introduced in the opening paragraph(s), and includes accompanying evidence which will show the thesis to be true.

Each body paragraph should have a single, thoroughly developed idea which stems from a subdivision of the thesis. Parts of the paragraph include:

1. Topic sentence which incorporates or introduces the subject of that paragraph or relates it to the thesis
2. Analysis or development of this topic sentence or concept
3. Evidence (any of the five types listed in previous outline)
4. A final sentence which anchors the evidence to the thesis and refreshes the reader's mind about the paper's purpose.

Analysis:

Analysis is simply a deeper consideration of the topic sentence, an extension of its thought, in the abstract. Examples of the topic sentence do not constitute analysis; examples are evidence (II.C).

The Analytic Gap:

A common flaw in many papers is that the student has skipped this second step, analysis, and has jumped to the more comfortable ground of presenting evidence, which is usually easier because it involves using a quote or narrating a bit of plot. Analytic writing tends to be more abstract, and requires a grasp of the larger concept. When this step is missing, it leaves an **analytic gap.** Be watchful for it in the first body paragraph, where it often appears.

Examples of Analytic Gap: In each of these passages, the question appearing below the sample paragraph must be answered after the topic sentence and before launching into the example or evidence.

Sample 1:

In *The Nun's Priest's Tale*, Chaucer illustrates the faults of courtly love. Chaunticleer, the rooster, loves one of the hens more than the others. When Chaunticleer tries to communicate with Pertilote, she chides him for not being a man.
GAP: What are the faults of courtly love? The writer has plunged right into characters and plot when he/she should list those faults of courtly love first.

Sample 2:

The author points out the contradiction in the role of knights and their codes of chivalry. On the front of Sir Gawain's shield, he had a five-pointed star representing five virtues: fellowship, generosity, pity, courtesy and chastity....
GAP: What is the contradiction? Right after sentence one, there should be a statement about how the role of all knights contradicts the code of chivalry.

Sample 3:

Hamlet's behavior reflects a code of ethics that is established throughout the play. First, the death of Old Hamlet raises the question of whether it was ethical for Hamlet to mourn for a long period of time.
GAP: What is the code of ethics established by the play?

In each case, the analytic gaps occur just after the first sentence. They happen when students rush ahead to the easier task of discussing story line or character before developing a deeper extension of the opening or topic sentence.

Here's an example of a partial paragraph **with analysis, no gap:** (Analysis is underlined.)

Brian Gilbert's ethics are based on the medieval ideal of chivalry that might makes right. <u>He feels that moral questions can be solved by force. He holds the belief that in battle or confrontation, God would give the strength to whomever He felt was right.</u> For example, when Rebecca is put on trial for sorcery, Gilbert's Order of Knights Templars commands that the only way her guilt or innocence can be decided is by the sword.

Evidence:

For each major point you make, you'll need evidence of one sort or another. If the question involved is controversial, you can, and in some cases should, give evidence on both sides and analyze which position is most worthy or convincing, and why. For most essays in a literature class, however, presentation of the evidence supporting only your thesis is probably sufficient. Check with your instructor.

Evidence can consist of these types:

1. Incident of plot. Beware of overdoing this. You only need to inform the reader of the elements in an incident that support the point you're making. Starting to tell an incident of plot often leads writers to continue telling the story beyond the single incident needed for development of a single point. Don't fall into this trap. Never feel compelled to inform the reader of the whole picture. You want him to focus on your argument, not on the narrative (story summary). Use present tense for this.

2. Character analysis. An examination of a character's attitudes based on actions, interior monologue (the character's thinking) and paraphrased dialogue can serve to support your thesis. Use the accumulation of details to support your claim, but be sure the reader knows what claim you are making about the character before you flood him with details. If you don't, your writing will exhibit an analytic gap.

3. Quotations. A common mistake is to plug in quotes without prefacing them with interpretive comment by you. Never abandon a quote or let it float on its own in your essay; always anchor it to your own analysis. Do not assume the reader will interpret it as you intend. Always indicate what each quote is illustrating and, when necessary, indicate the speaker. Always use quotation marks. Page numbers usually are not necessary, but for Greek and Shakespearean plays, use act, scene and line numbers in parenthesis, like this (III.iv.112-3).

See Section VI, "How to Handle Quotes."

4. Examination of symbolism, images or figurative language in the text of the literature. While it is naive to assume that authors write by "planting" symbols to give "hidden meaning," (please, don't use that simplistic term in your papers) it is often useful to consider what repeated or emphasized objects, words, actions, colors, sensory details, Biblical references and the like might suggest in relation to a work's thematic content. Even while referring to symbolism or imagery or figurative language as the basis for your paper's argument, it is best not to affirm what "the author meant." Instead, you might word it this way: "The recurring image of —— suggests...."

For definition of these terms, see the Glossary.

5. Historical and cultural background of the time period. Here is where you can draw on what you know outside the work of literature, as well as what the author suggests about the conditions, mores, attitudes, social problems, values, and movements contemporary to a work of literature. Be cautious of this, however. Historical background can be abused as an easy way out of supporting a claim that should be defensible from within the text as well. Using absolute or irrefutable arguments relative to the work's time period tends to cut short your examination and therefore ignores the timelessness of the work.

You may mix these types of evidence in your body paragraphs, using whatever is most appropriate.

Reanchoring for Unity:

An essay must contain parts that are all related. This is called cohesiveness or unity. It cannot be a loose collection of responses to the topic. Never let your reader lose sight of your thesis, even for the length of a sentence. Every paragraph, every bit of evidence must be tied closely to the main point of the entire paper. Do this by re-suggesting the main claim at the end of each body paragraph. Don't move from one subtopic to another, or from one body paragraph to another without anchoring each point to the thesis. Continually remind the reader of the thesis. Pile up evidence and hammer it home.

Keep in mind two additional considerations in writing the body: balance and order.

Balance:

In every paper, both evidence and ideas (concepts or interpretations of your own) are expected. A good paper exhibits a careful balance between the two. A paper with only examples and no thinking (no clearly stated points of interpretation) might be criticized for not analyzing the essay question. Conversely, a paper with brilliant or original interpretation and analysis, but lacking evidence, or with only vague support without quotations and specifics, will probably be criticized for not establishing the validity of your ideas.

Order:

Before beginning to write the body of your paper, you need to decide in what order to put the information. Are you going to save your most powerful point for the last or are you going to start with it? No single rule is applicable to all assignments, but whatever order is suggested by the thesis should be followed in the body of the paper. Are you going to cover the material chronologically, in the order in which the original narrative is told? If so, beware of the common trap of telling the whole story, including details unnecessary to your thesis. If the essay question consists of a series of questions, you could address each one in a separate paragraph; usually such questions follow some logic.

See Section III, "Common Types of Essay Questions," for a discussion of ordering a compare/contrast question.

C. Conclusion

The conclusion should be a separate paragraph or paragraphs. Do not tack it on as a single sentence at the end of the last paragraph of the body. An adequate conclusion restates the thesis, perhaps in different or stronger words; a better conclusion even goes beyond the question, saying something broader or deeper than what you started with in your thesis sentence, but without introducing an entirely new topic. A conclusion can contain a quotation but must not rely on it to carry the argument. It should give a definitive answer to the essay question. It should not tell the ending of the narrative since the purpose of the essay was not to give a plot summary, nor should it discuss details which have not been examined in the body.

Titles:

Titles should give a focus or imply a stance on a subject, not merely indicate the subject. Overly general titles are nearly useless. Titles are another opportunity to convey meaning. Don't throw away that opportunity to make your essay a strong one.

Above all, never use "essay" or "essay on" or "English," or the name of the course in your title. Never use the title of the original piece of literature as the title of your essay. That title has already been used, so it is not available to you. Besides, you're focusing on something about that work; you're not rewriting the work. You can, however, and many writers do, use the title of the original literary work as part of your title. Titles are often more effective if they employ alliteration or allusion. See Section XXIII, "Glossary of Literary Terms," for explanation. Some samples follow.

POOR:	BETTER:
Salem Witches (too bland)	Explosion of Hysteria in Salem (stronger word choice)
Revenge in Salem	Vengeance Walks in Salem (paraphrase of a quote)
The Renaissance (too general)	The Renaissance: Renewal of Discovery (indicates focus)
Gawain's Decision (too general)	Gawain's Grave Dilemma (uses alliteration)
Hamlet's Moral Obligation	Hamlet as Scourge and Minister (uses allusion)
Shakespeare's Imagery (too general)	Disease Imagery in <u>Hamlet</u>

Punctuation of Titles:

Original titles (those made up by you) should have no punctuation (no underline and no quotation marks). If, however, your title incorporates or includes the title of a piece of literature, then only that original title should carry punctuation, as in the last example above.

If it is a full length play (three acts or more), a novel, book or magazine, then underline it. If it is a short story, one-act play, poem, article, or anything originally published within a larger work carrying its own title, then use quotation marks around that portion of your title. Like this:

> Irony in "A Modest Proposal"
> The Racial Question in <u>Huckleberry Finn</u>
> <u>East of Eden</u>: Brotherly Jealousy Revisited

Movies should always be underlined.

Italics can always be substituted for an underline but never for quotation marks.

SECTION III.

COMMON TYPES OF ESSAY QUESTIONS

Usually essay questions are written utilizing a key word which gives you direction in structuring your essay. Here are some commonly used key words and some advice about each:

Compare: Look for characteristics that resemble each other. Emphasize similarities, but in some cases also mention differences.

Contrast: Stress the dissimilarities of the items or works.

For further discussion of **compare/contrast** essays, see p. 12-13.

Criticize: Express your judgment about the merit of a work or the truth of a concept.

Define: Give a concise, clear meaning for the topic and follow through with its sub-points or your reasoning.

Describe: Recount, characterize, sketch, narrate or relate in sequence.

Discuss: Examine, analyze carefully, and give reasons for opinions. Include related material.

Evaluate: Carefully appraise the work, citing both its merits and limitations. You might include the appraisal of authorities in addition to your own.

Interpret: Give a line by line interpretation or analysis if the work is a short poem; otherwise, comment on the suggestions, meaning or messages in a given work. "Give a reading of" means to interpret or comment on every significant line. This is often done for a soliloquy in Shakespeare, for a sonnet or other relatively short poem.

Review: Examine a subject critically, analyzing and commenting on its important parts.

Summarize: Give the main points or facts in condensed form, omitting the details and illustrations. This is often called a precis.

Trace: In narrative or chronological order, describe the progress or development of the topic.

Although not every essay question you may encounter necessarily falls into an identifiable category, some do. When that happens, recognizing that category may aid in answering the question directly. Here are three common varieties of questions on literature.

A. CHARACTER ANALYSIS:

Although the word "character" sometimes means "person," or "literary figure," it also means an individual's personal qualities and characteristics, which may include his moral code, his fears and limitations, his mental conflicts, his ideals, values, and motivations. All of these should be considered when writing a character analysis.

Be aware of these ways in which a writer can indicate the character of his characters. He can unfold character:

1. By what the character himself says and/or thinks.
2. By what other characters say or feel about him.
3. By what the character does and does not do.
4. By what the narrator reveals about him directly.

Considering all of these may give you ways to support your general analysis.

It's also important to consider whether the character is static or developing. A static character usually remains the same—has the same attitudes, abilities, morals at the end of the piece of literature as he does at the beginning. If you are permitted to choose a character to analyze, you may find you have less to say about a static character. A developing character, however, undergoes some change. He grows. He reaches a new level of understanding. Perhaps this growth occurs through a painful experience. If you choose a developing character to analyze, be sure to consider this growth and its causes as a possible focus of your commentary.

One thing you must avoid when tracing the growth of a character is the trap of the plot summary. Only refer to incidents of plot that reflect the various stages of growth. Do not include irrelevant information or plot items that the author had to include in order to get from one time to another in his narrative. Giving an entire plot summary is just about the worst thing you can do in answer to a character analysis question.

B. COMPARISON/CONTRAST:

An instructor may ask you to compare two works by the same author, two authors or two characters. He may assign the two topics, or he may want you to select two works or two characters that make a good comparison. In any case, it is your job to find what is similar (that's the "compare" part of the question) and what is dissimilar (the "contrast" part) about the two.

You may be asked for a general comparison, or for an examination of only one aspect of the two authors or works. For example, you may be asked to compare Hemingway's characterization of women in *A Farewell to Arms* to *The Sun Also Rises*. A question may ask for a comparison of imagery in Frost's poem "Birches" to "After Apple Picking." You may be asked to compare Scout Finch's recollections of a time of significant growth in *To Kill a Mockingbird* to Gene's recollection of a similar time of growth for him in *A Separate Peace*. In any case, this type of question directs you to focus on one area in two works and thereby come to understand each work more deeply.

It is easier to begin compare/contrast essays by settling first on an organizational plan. There are two possible approaches. You may divide your topic into subtopics and then treat each subtopic, first considering it in relation to X and then considering it in relation to Y. An outline of this plan would look like this:

I. Introduction and thesis

II. Subtopic One:
   A. Work (or author) X
   B. Work (or author) Y

III. Subtopic Two:
   A. Work (or author) X
   B. Work (or author) Y

IV. Subtopic Three:
   A. Work (or author) X
   B. Work (or author) Y

V. Conclusion

You can readily see that this approach, if used when there are more than three subtopics, quickly becomes a "ping pong ball" method, bouncing the reader back and forth between the two. In doing so, the writer's tendency is often to race too quickly through each point without developing it. It may be better to develop fully one side of the comparison first, and then the other. An outline for such an approach will look like this:

I. Introduction and thesis

II. Work (or author) X
   A. Subtopic A
   B. Subtopic B
   C. Subtopic C

III. Work (or author) Y
   A. Subtopic A
   B. Subtopic B
   C. Subtopic C

IV. Conclusion

Most assignments will not be so long that the reader will forget what you said about subtopic A for work X by the time you get to work Y. This encourages depth, but let that also be a warning. If the essay is to be done under timed conditions in a class period, divide the time equally between X and Y so the second one doesn't get shortchanged.

C. AGREE/DISAGREE:

An agree/disagree essay question may contain (1) a statement posed by the instructor, (2) a quotation evaluating or criticizing an author or work of literature, or (3) a quotation direct from a primary source (the piece of literature itself). In either case, you are asked to agree or disagree with the statement and then defend your stance. You should never be afraid to disagree, IF you can think of strong arguments.

Most likely, your first paragraph will contain the quotation and its source (if other than a statement made up just for the occasion of the assignment), and your thesis statement attacking it or defending it. Then the body of your paper heaps up reasons or examples suggesting that the quotation is valid or invalid. Here are some sample agree-disagree questions of each variety:

Type 1: Willy Loman succeeds as a tragic hero because he touches man's universal fear of failure. Agree or disagree.

Note: Essential to a complete answer to this question is a definition of a tragic hero. That should probably be included in the opening paragraph so that the rest of your essay can be tied to it. Often such a definition of terms is required by an essay. It's better to use a definition formulated in class discussion or lecture, or one obtained from a literary glossary rather than one from a dictionary which usually yields only a superficial definition.

Type 2: Agree or disagree with this evaluation of Ralph Waldo Emerson from the *Southern Literary Messenger*, April 1861: "Your fragmentary philosopher, of the Emerson stamp, who disturbs the beliefs of the common folk, without again composing or attempting to compose them with a higher and purer faith, is a curse to society....He is a moral nuisance."

Note: Consider the geographical source and the date. Inclusion of such detail in the question suggests the importance of considering the intellectual climate of the time in the South.

Type 3: Hamlet tells Rosencrantz and Guildernstern, "There is nothing either good or bad, but thinking makes it so." Do you agree or disagree with his statement? In what circumstances is it true and when is it untrue?

Note: This type of question allows you to go beyond the play to discuss a concept, leaving you free to consider that concept in light of your own experience or observations from history or the contemporary world. Not doing so would offer less than what was asked for.

SECTION IV.

PROCEDURES FOR WRITING ESSAYS

There are many approaches to the task of writing a critical essay. No single method is necessarily right for all people. For some, writing a detailed outline is helpful; for others only a list of phrases, each representing the topic of a paragraph, may be all that is needed. Those who find it difficult to write the opening sentence can start instead with the first paragraph of the body and then return to write the introduction. Any of these approaches can be tried.

If you feel more secure working from an outline or series of topics, you might also consider indicating on the outline what evidence you intend to use for each major point. By listing the points first, then by attaching some evidence to each point, you may be able to avoid the trap of retelling the narrative of the original literature. By using this method, you will have thought out the whole essay first, before you begin writing your opening paragraph. Then the actual writing process is easier because you don't need to panic at the end of each sentence or paragraph, wondering where you're going next.

One approach some teachers suggest, called clustering, consists of writing in the middle of a page the single word or phrase which is the topic of your paper, and then surrounding it with related ideas or subpoints, each in a circle attached to the central idea like spokes of a wheel. This might be helpful when the topic is open ended.

For the topic, "Examine the social criticism of Mark Twain in *Huckleberry Finn*," a cluster might look like this:

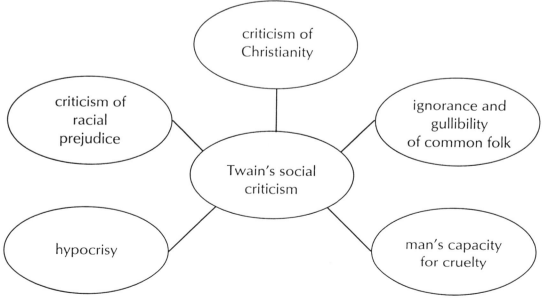

Attached to each circle would be another circle giving an example from the novel which illustrates each point. Then the writing process would involve first addressing the item in the center and then each spoke of the wheel with its accompanying proof.

For the topic, "What is Nathaniel Hawthorne's code of morality as expressed in *The Scarlet Letter*?" the clustering might look like this:

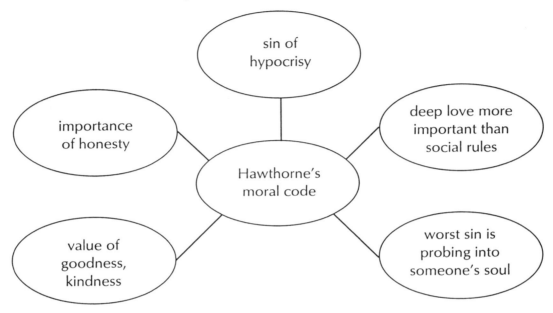

Another approach might be to make a chart with the thesis of your essay across the top, and subtopics down the left side, with an explanation, plot example, related character, and quote for each. That might look like this:

THESIS: Twain's criticism of pre-Civil War America in *Huckleberry Finn* centers on human ignorance as expressed in racial prejudice and hypocrisy, as well as moral offenses such as the abuse of Christianity and human cruelty.

subtopic	explanation or analysis	plot example	related character	quote
racial prejudice				
ignorance and gullibility				
middle class hypocrisy				
abuse of Christianity				
man's capacity for cruelty				

Column headings may vary based on what the essay requires. For example, an essay question might be, "In what ways did the Renaissance establish a set of attitudes different than the Middle Ages?" The chart might look like this:

THESIS: Because of the growth of optimism and a move away from rigid Christianity of the Middle Ages, the Renaissance established a renewal of learning and an expansion of human potential evident in all areas of man's experience and thinking.

subtopic	discarded attitude	new attitude	event or movement	person	date
philosophy					
religion					
science					
geography					
art					
literature					

Whichever method you use, be sure that your writing is in direct answer to the question. However intelligent and perceptive your writing is, if it does not address the question asked, it does not meet the assignment. Pull out the core words of the question and underline them. Keep rereading the question while you are framing your answer. Often essay questions have many parts. You must address all parts; each part should be developed in a separate paragraph or more. In this case, your thesis and your conclusion should address the larger issue which serves as an umbrella over the sub-parts.

As you do the first draft, do not be concerned with points of mechanics such as spelling, punctuation, grammar. This often distracts from the thought process of getting down the idea. If you are not sure of the spelling of a word, or of a word's meaning, just make a guess and go on. Do not interrupt the flow of ideas. Then go back, after you finish the draft, to consider items such as word choice, grammar, sentence construction.

At some point after the first draft is completed, you may wish to consult a thesaurus to find a more appropriate word. If you do, be careful that you don't choose a word so elevated in style or so obscure that it stands out as different from your normal style. It's best to use a thesaurus to remind yourself of words that are already in your recognition vocabulary but just didn't come to mind when you were grappling with a concept. Be extremely careful of using a word which is brand new to you. Check yourself by consulting a dictionary for a word the thesaurus gives you to make sure it means exactly what you need.

When you complete a first draft which you feel addresses the question directly and completely, evaluate your work according to two measures—the sections called "How to Revise and Edit" and "On Achieving a More Sophisticated Style."

The final procedure is to tighten. Most student papers can cut one fourth of the words and not lose meaning. Do not use a phrase where a well-chosen word will do. Tighter essays are always stronger. Length is no guarantee of excellence. See Section VIII, "Tightening Your Writing," to learn how to distinguish between necessary and unnecessary parts of your sentences. This is the final polishing. Don't skip it. It can make the difference between an "A" and a "B."

HOW TO STATE A THEME

The theme of a piece of literature is the author's message or attitude toward a universal topic, something more timeless than the exact situation of the characters. Realize that most pieces of literature illustrate more than one attitude so there usually is a multiplicity of themes, particularly in a novel or a full length play. There is a danger in taking an arbitrary stance by insisting that one particular concept is THE theme of a work.

Likewise, avoid the tone which implies that an author seeks to "hide" a single "message" in a story as if he is playing hide-and-go-seek with the reader. Use of the term "hidden meaning" is a holdover from junior high which should be dropped.

Do not confuse theme with thesis. In the context of a literature class, a thesis is an argument or proposition you intend to illustrate or develop in an essay. Theme generally refers to an attitude from literature itself, not from an essay commenting on literature.

If an assignment asks you to state the theme of a piece of literature, follow these guidelines:

1. A theme is a complete thought in a full sentence with subject, verb and complement. You need to do more than simply indicate a topic only. A topic is a single word or phrase like jealousy, the institution of marriage, racial hatred, maturity. These topics need to be developed into a complete sentence that indicates the author's attitude about these issues.

POOR: The author's message is about racial hatred.

BETTER: One of author's messages is that racial hatred exists where there is fear of an unknown group of people.

Note the change from "about" to "that." "About" introduces only a topic. "That" leads the writer to introduce a fuller theme stated in a sentence.

POOR: The theme of the novel is growing up.

BETTER: One theme is that painful experiences often force young people to grow up quickly.

2. Most good statements of theme make an observation about life, human beings, human relationships, morality, civilization, justice or some other broad topic which is seen as universally true. The author uses characters to show us something *about* life or people. Dig until you uncover what the author feels about his broad topic, not just about his characters.

3. It's best not to refer to details, characters, events of plot, or setting in your single sentence statement of theme. Generalize. What the author wants us to come away with is a new feeling, attitude, or insight that can be related to life outside the piece of literature.

Be aware that this rule applies to thematic statements (statements of the author's message), not thesis statements responding to specific essay questions which may require you to focus on a single character.

4. State the author's message as an idea, an observation on humanity, life, or whatever the broad topic is. It should not be stated as advice.

POOR: The author's message is to keep trying, no matter what the odds.

BETTER: The author asserts that when individuals don't give up, even though faced by fearful odds, they will eventually find satisfaction.

POOR: Don't judge another culture by the standards of your own.

BETTER: The poem suggests that when confronted by a different culture, it is most fair to disregard one's own cultural standards and values in order to look at the new culture without preconceived ideas.

SECTION VI.

HOW TO HANDLE QUOTES

Practically every essay written on a literary topic could be strengthened by more effective use of quotes from the text or primary source, which means the literature itself.

Quotes generally need to be accompanied by three pieces of information:

a. Identification of speaker

b. Indication of situation (very brief)

c. Interpretation or commentary on substance of quote, especially in relation to topic sentence and/or thesis.

A common mismanagement of quotes occurs because the quote is unexplained; the writer assumes his readers (or the instructor) will interpret it as he intends. The quote is left floating, without introduction of who is speaking, and often without explanation as to what is being illustrated. Instead, the writer jumps from his topic sentence directly to his quotation, skipping essential interpretation of the topic sentence. Such mismanagement might look like this:

Heroism in *Beowulf* consists of remaining loyal to one's fellow man. "Beowulf, my friend! So you have come here because of past favours, to fight in our behalf."

In this example, we don't know who is speaking, and we need to be told that this quotation illustrates loyalty expressed in a situation of dire social need. Such an interpretive comment can come before or after the quotation, but it MUST be somewhere. Here is an improved version:

Heroism in *Beowulf* consists of remaining loyal to one's fellow man, an essential ingredient in the Anglo-Saxon society in which survival depended upon group solidarity, particularly in situations of dire social need or natural or supernatural threats. Hrothgar commends Beowulf by saying, "Beowulf, my friend! So you have come here because of past favours, to fight in our behalf." By coming to protect his fellow humans against the ferocious monster, Beowulf displays the heroic quality of loyalty.

(Note the preferred use of present tense here.)

Students often skip these essential steps of analysis of the topic sentence and interpretation of the quotation because analysis is harder to write. They often don't know what needs to be said, and find it much easier just to rely on the quote alone to support their topic sentence Remember that the outline of body paragraphs (page 3) calls for these steps: topic sentence, analysis, then evidence. If that evidence is a quote, the quote itself requires analytic commentary. Leaving gaps in analysis often makes a difference between an adequate and an outstanding paper. (See Analytic Gap, p. 6-7.)

Here is another example from a student essay on Steinbeck's novel, *The Pearl*, with the analytical commentary, (II.b. on essay format outline, page 3) missing:

> Steinbeck suggests that the desire for riches, as represented by the pearl, can ruin
>
> a person's life.
>
>> And in the surface of the pearl he saw Coyotito lying in the little cave with the top of his head shot away. And the pearl was ugly; it was gray, like a malignant growth. And Kino heard the music of the pearl, distorted and insane.

A better version would include these additions:

> Steinbeck suggests that the desire for riches, as represented by the pearl, can ruin
>
> a person's life so drastically that what was previously seen as beautiful becomes
>
> tarnished and evil. After the jealousy, greed and materialism of the community
>
> ripens into injustice, and Kino and Juana lose their house and child in the fight to
>
> convert the pearl to income, they seek to throw it away. At this point, Steinbeck
>
> describes it as a thing detestable:
>
>> And in the surface of the pearl he saw Coyotito lying in the little cave with the top of his head shot away. And the pearl was ugly; it was gray, like a malignant growth. And Kino heard the music of the pearl, distorted and insane.

This fuller version not only gives more analysis, but sets the quotation in context. It should be followed by a sentence reanchoring the paragraph to the paper's thesis. Note again the correct use of present tense for textual commentary.

Sometimes, an interpretive comment need not be a separate sentence. An essay on *Walden* by Henry David Thoreau might contain the following, which combines interpretation and quote in a single sentence:

> Thoreau's idea that men devote their lives to unworthy goals is shown when he writes, "The mass of men lead lives of quiet desperation."

Identification of the speaker in that case is not necessary because the work is clearly autobiographical, with Thoreau narrating his own experience. When a character rather than a narrator expresses an idea, it's important to indicate who said it. An essay on Hawthorne's *The Scarlet Letter* might contain this:

Dimmesdale voices Hawthorne's implied condemnation of Chillingworth when Dimmesdale tells Hester:

> We are not, Hester, the worst sinners in the world. There is one worse than even the polluted priest! That old man's revenge has been blacker than my sin. He has violated, in cold blood, the sanctity of a human heart.

The student writer should continue this paragraph with his own interpretation of the "violation of the sanctity of a human heart."

An effective style of giving evidence is to embed short phrases from the original literature into interpretive sentences of your own design. Such an approach for an essay on *Beowulf* might look like this:

> The author observes that in times of fear or anger, the people mix their old pagan gods and superstitions with the new Christianity. They believe that fate brought "this cursed creature," Grendel, upon them. Yet even here the Christian concept of evil is evident. Grendel is said to be a "hellish fiend" who was condemned by God "as one of the seed of Cain," out of revenge for Abel's death.

Do not include the words "quote" or "quotation" in your essay. You don't need to introduce a quotation by calling it one. The sentence, "Emerson tells his opinion in the following quotation," is wasted and annoying. Instead, identify the opinion and get right to the quote. Like this: "Emerson's criticism of conformity is evident in 'Self Reliance' when he writes..." and then insert the quote.

Never write: "When Huck comes back to the hiding place on Jackson's Island, he quotes, 'Get up and hump yourself, Jim; they're after us.'" Huck didn't quote it. Neither did Twain. You did. Just use, "Huck says."

MECHANICS OF HANDLING QUOTES: Quotations of less than four lines are typed in the general text which is double-spaced. Quotations of four lines or more (at least 40 words) are indented at right and left margin and single-spaced, without quotation marks. An essay on Shakespeare's *As You Like It* may contain something like this:

Jacques demonstrates his ability to step back from the present situation and comment upon it when he gives his "seven ages of man" speech:

> All the world's a stage,
> And all the men and women merely players:
> They have their exits and their entrances;
> And one man in his time plays many parts,
> His acts being seven ages (II.vii.139-143).

He shows his pessimism by saying in the seventh stage, man ends up like a child in old age, just as dependent and helpless as an infant.

When quoting only two or three lines from poetry, or from a verse portion of a play, use a slash mark to indicate where the lines are split in the original. Since it is less than four lines, it is not indented. It looks like this:

In his soliloquy, Claudius demonstrates that he is not an amoral murderer without

remorse. He says, "O, my offence is rank, it smells to heaven;/It hath the primal

eldest curse upon't;/A brother's murder," (III.iii.36-8).

Be sure to keep the original capitalization and punctuation. When quoting from Shakespearean or Greek plays, and when the play is identified elsewhere in the essay, always cite the quote by referring to act, scene and line number in parenthesis after the quote but before the period. As illustrated above, use periods between act, scene and line numbers. Do not use page numbers since texts may differ.

Check with your instructor about requirements for citing line numbers for poetry.

HOW TO REVISE AND EDIT

Revising and editing is a necessary step in all good writing. The student who just gives his essays a quick once-over, looking for all grammatical, spelling and word choice errors at the same time that he reads for style and content, does himself a disservice. Such a student will never know how well he can write because he hasn't isolated separate aspects of his writing in order to improve each one.

Revision refers to reconsidering the content and the organization of the paper, while editing refers to correction of style, word usage, grammar, punctuation and proofreading. It's asking too much to do all of this at the same time. Students should edit papers several times, each time considering only one type of improvement.

For content revision, consider these points:

1. Have I answered the question directly both in the thesis as well as the body of the paper, or have I just written vaguely about the topic? Does the thesis or claim merely repeat the information in the question, or does it provide a substantial answer?

2. Have I addressed all parts of a multiple-part question?

3. Is each major point supported by evidence? See Section II, B, p. 6-8.

4. Is the paper free of irrelevant information not asked for in the essay question and not useful as support of the thesis?

5. Does the paper have unsupported generalities?

6. Are quotations interpreted? Is the relationship between the quote and the topic sentence of its paragraph clear?

7. Have I left any analytic gaps, where I have jumped from the topic sentence to examples? See p. 6-7.

8. Do my ideas show maturity of vision, depth, a large world view, an examination of underlying moral issues and universal human concerns?

9. Is the title strong, appealing, indicative of the stance of the paper? See p. 9-10.

To evaluate organization and revise where needed, consider the following:

1. Do I have a clearly identifiable thesis statement or claim in the opening paragraph?
2. Does the argument set forth in the body of the paper match and directly support the claim?
3. Is each separate idea developed fully in a paragraph of its own with a clearly identifiable topic sentence?
4. Do I have transitions between each separate idea?
5. Do I keep the thesis clearly in mind during all the paragraphs of the body? Are all paragraphs of the body anchored to the thesis?
6. Do I conclude the paper with a restatement of the original thesis, or, better yet, do I restate the original thesis and go on with an even more insightful point?

For style editing, consider the following:

1. Is my writing vivid? Do I use precise word choices and original expressions?
2. Is it enjoyable to read? Does it have personality?
3. Is the writing tight? Have I used a phrase to say what can be said in a word? See Section VIII, on how to tighten.
4. Have I avoided all cliches? See Section X.
5. Search for the points listed in Section IX, On Achieving a More Sophisticated Style, especially diction shifts, use of first and second person, and present tense for references to literary text.

For mechanical editing, the task may be divided into several readings. In each reading, check for one of the following:

1. Spelling of unusual words. A spell checker on a word precessing computer program is only partially helpful. It will not identify misspellings which create a different word.
2. Spelling of common words that always give you trouble, the ones that always make you hesitate. It's a good idea to keep an alphabetized list of these personally troublesome words.
3. Fragments, especially common when sentences begin with "because" and "that." See Section XV. It's helpful to read papers aloud when looking for fragments. Separate each sentence from the one preceding it and the one following it. Do not connect them in your mind and do not read smoothly from one sentence to the next. For each sentence, pause and ask if it can stand alone without any other sentence around it. Does it need another sentence read with it to make sense? If it does, then it's likely to be a sentence fragment. If you can't mentally separate each sentence from the one previous, read sentences in reverse order. This will force you to look at each sentence individually.

4. Run-ons, especially common when a comma is followed by a new subject and a new verb. See Section XVI.

5. Lack of parallel construction, especially common in any series of three or more items, each with a different structure or beginning with a different part of speech. See Section XVII, part 4.

6. Agreement errors, especially common when a word like *everyone, someone, anybody* is followed by verb and then a pronoun which should be "his" but is often written incorrectly as "their." See Section XIV.

7. Closure on quotation marks.

8. Usage errors. Consult Section XI, Usage. Often these are word pairs that confuse us. Be cautious about words that sound alike but are spelled differently, like "there" and "their," "accept" and "except." Keep a list of usage errors you have made in the past and check for them in each new piece of writing you do.

9. If the title of the paper includes a title of a literary work, is it punctuated correctly? (Underline for book, play, epic poem; quotation marks for short story, poem, essay.)

TIGHTENING YOUR WRITING

Tight writing is concise. Because unnecessary words have been trimmed, the remaining language is bold, direct and much more precise than loosely worded sentences which use a phrase where a single word would do.

Few writers write tightly on their first drafts, but good writers always eliminate dead words and phrases—those that communicate little meaning—and examine every idea to determine if it can be said more concisely. If it can, the result is harder hitting, more effective.

Tightening your writing is done by repeated editing, by looking for the core words in every sentence, strengthening them, and trimming around them.

Here are some strategies:

1. Eliminate these common filler words and phrases in most formal academic writing, particularly in literary criticism:

> I think
> It seems to me that
> It appears that
> It is clear that
> It is my opinion that
> What happened was that
> He was a writer who
> How this works is
> What that means is
> What I want to say is
> The author is trying to say that

Usually your sentence should start with the next word. Watch for these fillers by questioning what comes before every "that" used as a conjunction joining two sentences.

2. Sometimes a word or shorter phrase can replace a longer phrase. For example:

POOR:	BETTER:
The reason why is that	because
In many cases, the students were	many students were
This problem is a difficult one.	This problem is difficult.
This is an idea that	This idea
There is no question that	Certainly,

the question about whether	whether
the society in which he lived	his society
available for lending purposes	available to lend
each and every	every
the number one cause of	the major cause of
at this point in time	now
in close proximity	near
has the capacity of	can
present a picture similar to	resemble
even though that is true	nevertheless
time and time again	frequently
his thoughts and feelings	his attitudes
the world around us	the world
his inner happiness	his happiness
positive inspiration	inspiration
self pride	pride
his fate and destiny	his fate
I myself have done this.	I have done this.

3. Eliminating a phrase of bland words in favor of a more dynamic single word sharpens meaning as well as tightens word count:

POOR:	BETTER:
the thing I want to do most	my passion
the thing I hate most	my aversion
the terrible thing that happened to her	her tragedy
his inability to pass the class and his lack of interest in the subject matter	his failure and apathy
the grumpy look on her face	her sullen expression
the embarrassment and shame he faced in front of everyone	his public disgrace
choose some to throw away	eliminate some

Substituting single words for wordy phrases focuses the reader's attention where you want it, on the core of your meaning, not on the stepping stones to get there. More dynamic words will make your sentences more memorable. Notice that the wordy phrases often contain a verb or a prepositional phrase (on her face, in front of everyone) where the concise ones do not.   Consider how much stronger the tightened sentence is in this example:

POOR: Hrothgar and Beowulf are two examples of how men should conduct themselves.
BETTER: Hrothgar and Beowulf exemplify ideal human conduct.

4. A particularly troublesome phrase is "the fact that." Always try to avoid it.

POOR:	BETTER:
in spite of the fact that	despite, although
I was unaware of the fact that	I was unaware that
because of the fact that	because
the fact that he said	his statement
the fact that he had not yet arrived	his lateness
the fact that he hated people unlike himself	his bigotry

Note: In the last three examples the more concise correction uses a noun instead of a subject and verb. Doing this will help to avoid a long series of short words.

5. Eliminate superfluous adjectives, adverbs and other qualifiers:

very, kind of, just, almost, always, really, only, yet, even, a lot of, usually, rather, some, still, so, somewhat, a wide variety of.

6. Shorten long verb forms:

POOR:	BETTER:
She will be leaving.	She will leave.
He is planning on beginning to study.	He intends to study.
He is going to go to college.	He will go to college.

7. Use appositives instead of "who is" and "which is." An appositive is a phrase, usually without a verb, which explains or identifies the previous noun in a sentence.

POOR: Thomas Hardy, who was the son of a stone mason, was denied admission to Oxford University.

BETTER: Thomas Hardy, the son of a stone mason, was denied admission to Oxford University.

Note: The phrase between commas is the appositive and must have commas before and after it.

POOR: *Huckleberry Finn*, which I feel is Twain's major work, was published in 1885.

BETTER: *Huckleberry Finn*, Twain's major work, was published in 1885.

8. **Overlapping Sentences:** Wordiness is sometimes caused by repetition and overlapping phrases. Reword sentences that do not move the reader forward a significant amount because they must repeat some element contained in the previous sentence. Underlines indicate those repeated ideas in these examples:

POOR: In order for a human group to achieve the level of civilization, the individuals <u>who make up that group</u> must have common beliefs and values. They must hold <u>common</u> goals even though <u>those goals</u> might not be achieved.

BETTER: For a group to achieve the level of civilization, its individuals must have common beliefs, values and goals.

POOR: There were many problems that contributed to the French Revolution. <u>Two major problems</u> were poverty, and corruption of the nobility.

BETTER: Of the many problems contributing to the French Revolution, poverty and corruption of the nobility were major factors.

POOR: The main part of the Ancient Mariner's retribution is to pay with "life in death." He must <u>live forever</u> and tell his tale. <u>Telling his tale</u> is necessary because it is the only thing that rids him of his pain.

BETTER: The Ancient Mariner's retribution consists primarily of paying with "life in death," by telling his tale forever in order to rid him of his pain.

Sometimes an entire paragraph must be restructured:

POOR: Huckleberry Finn has some difficult decisions to make about Jim. Jim is a Negro slave who is escaping from his owner. Huck and Jim become friends because Huck is escaping civilization too, so they float south on a raft together. In a different way, Huck wants freedom just as much as Jim does, so Huck wants to help Jim escape because Jim has been kind to him. Helping a slave escape was against the Fugitive Slave Law. It is also against what Huck was taught by the Widow Douglas. Huck is afraid of what Tom Sawyer would think of him if he helped Jim. He struggles with this problem all the time they were heading south.
(116 words; 8 sentences)

BETTER: While floating south on a raft with his new friend Jim, an escaping Negro slave, Huckleberry struggles with two moral dilemmas—whether or not to go against the influence of the Widow Douglas and Tom Sawyer, and whether to disobey the Fugitive Slave Law by helping Jim escape. Their similar desires for freedom and Jim's kindness to Huck make him wrestle with the decision for a long time.
(68 words; 2 sentences)

ON ACHIEVING A MORE SOPHISTICATED STYLE

These stylistic suggestions will make your critical essays, reports and academic writing sound more sophisticated.

1. Avoid **cliches** which are trite, overused phrases. Expressions like "live life to its fullest" are dull word packages which demonstrate a lack of precise thinking and originality on the part of the writer. A partial list of such unimaginative phrases is contained in Section X, "Cliches."

2. The use of **first person** in literary criticism, that is, the use of "I think" or "I feel" or "in my opinion," is usually unnecessary, distracting and obvious. Some instructors are more flexible than others. Check first.

POOR: I like Frost's poetry because he makes you feel or see what a place is like.

BETTER: Frost uses the senses of feeling, hearing and seeing effectively to describe a place.

3. Avoid use of **second person** in essays of literary criticism. Second person is "you." It's not grammatically wrong, and the writing of correspondence and instructions usually demands it, but in academic writing it is out of place and unsophisticated. The use of "you" probably doesn't refer to the reader anyway. You mean people in general, so use "one," "people," "society," "most adults" or a similar term.

Note that the improved example in item 2 (above) eliminated the second person.

POOR: In Anglo-Saxon times, when you killed someone in battle or in an argument, you had to support his wife and family.

BETTER: In Anglo-Saxon times, when a man killed someone in battle or in an argument, he had to support the dead man's wife and family.

4. Avoid **overly general terms** such as good, bad, nice, very, really, quite, somewhat, rather, kind of. They do not show you to be a precise thinker or an imaginative writer. "He is a good man" could mean practically anything. Use a more specific term: ethical, kind, honest, sincere, industrious. When you want to stress an adjective by using very, as in "He was very sad," select a stronger adjective: "He was despondent," or "He was sorrowful."

5. Use a variety of **transitions** to link one idea or sub-topic to another. Such transitions may be phrases or words such as: on the contrary, however, in addition, on the other hand, similarly, above all, nevertheless, in spite of. Avoid, "in conclusion" and "to sum it up."

6. As a general rule, keep things in the same **tense** throughout the essay. If you start by giving examples from a narrative in the present tense, (the preferred tense for critical essays) do not switch to past tense unless you have a good reason to do so.

7. Avoid using the term "**a lot**." Substitute something more specific, or, if that is impossible, use "a great deal," or "many." Those terms are more sophisticated. (Note that "a lot" is two words, never one.)

8. In most cases, use **active voice** rather than passive. It's more direct and vigorous than the passive.

PASSIVE:	The cow was hit by a road-grader.
ACTIVE:	He hit the cow with a road-grader.
PASSIVE:	My first trip to New York will always be remembered by me.
ACTIVE:	I'll always remember my first trip to New York.
PASSIVE:	The reason he quit college was his poor health.
ACTIVE:	Poor health was the reason he quit college.
PASSIVE:	I was kissed by him.
ACTIVE:	He kissed me.

If you desire a narrative tone, use active, particularly for a personal essay. If you want a businesslike, objective or expository tone, sometimes the passive works better. These two sentences about Arthur Miller are equally effective:

PASSIVE: The issues of revenge, hysteria and hypocrisy within a rigid Puritan community are examined by Arthur Miller in *The Crucible*.
ACTIVE: In *The Crucible*, Arthur Miller examines the issues of revenge, hysteria and hypocrisy as they appear in a rigid Puritan community.

In this case, consider which part of the sentence you want to give prominence to.

9. For a direct style, put statements in **positive form.**

POOR: He was not often on time.

BETTER: He was usually late.

POOR: It was not uncommon to see him take an evening walk.

BETTER: It was common to see him take an evening walk.

The second item in each pair is preferable:

not honest	dishonest
not important	petty, unimportant, trifling
did not remember	forgot
did not pay any attention to	ignored

did not have much confidence in   distrusted

A side effect of putting statements in the positive form is conciseness, which usually makes your writing stronger. If you wish a highly literary tone, imitating academic critics, you might find a double negative stylistically effective, as in the following example:

It was not uncommon for Emily Dickinson to devise her own punctuation rules which made heavy use of the dash.

10. Always **be specific**. Vague writing is a common weakness in beginning writers and is the basis for feeling dissatisfied with your work. The writer who says, "I know what I want to say, but I just can't get it down on paper," probably does **not** know what he wants to say. He hasn't done enough precise thinking about his topic yet. To express thoroughly and precisely every point you introduce, look for words that generalize or group things together or words that give only a category of items rather than the items themselves. Such vague generalizations are underlined in the following examples:

POOR: Brad didn't like any of the traditions and activities of his high school. (What traditions and activities? What was wrong with them?)

BETTER: Brad thought the worn out high school traditions of football games, pep rallies and class competitions were trite, repetitious and silly.

POOR: The book is about the concept of civilization. (What's the concept?)

BETTER: The book explores the concept that civilization consists of a code of law or morality, a shared culture of the arts and a set of religious views.

POOR: One of the things in medieval life that Chaucer criticized was the church. (What about the church?)

BETTER: Two aspects of medieval life that Chaucer criticized were the materialism and corruption of the church.

BEST: Several aspects of the medieval church that Chaucer criticized were its materialism, corruption, strict hierarchy, and excessive ritual.

POOR: The experience taught me a great deal about life that I may not have learned otherwise. (What was the experience? What exactly did it teach you?)

BETTER: The death of my friend has taught me to value each day for its potential and cherish each person in my life for his or her good qualities.

In the above example, the cause of the poor writing in the first statement is the word "about." It usually leads to vagueness. Instead of using a verb, followed by "about," and then a noun or phrase ("taught me about life"), use the verb "taught" followed by an infinitive verb ("taught me to value…to cherish").

Similar vague words to avoid are:

> this, that, it, thing, some

> feelings, emotions, thoughts, beliefs, issues, problems
> (Name them; don't group together without identifying.)

> society (Too general; explain what aspect or forces or practices of society you mean

> how, as in "how they lived" or "how he thought" (Explain how he did think.)

11. Use **vivid word choice.** Make the reader see what you're imagining by using specific, concrete detail.

> cedars and pines, not trees
> jealousy and hypocrisy, not evil characteristics

Instead of saying a character or author "didn't like" something, explain precisely what he thought of that thing.

POOR: He didn't like any of the traditions and rituals of his religion.

BETTER: He thought his Old World religious rituals of christening, confirmation and confessions were useless and hypocritical.

12. **Keep related words together** to avoid misunderstanding.

POOR: Twain, in the nineteenth chapter of *Huckleberry Finn*, gives a description of a day on the Mississippi River.

BETTER: In the nineteenth chapter of *Huckleberry Finn*, Twain gives a description of...

POOR: The author of the biography of Lincoln, who... (Whom do you mean, Lincoln or the author?)

BETTER: Lincoln's biographer who...

Sometimes an error in word order results in absurdity, as in this example:

An explosion and fire destroyed an apartment building in Boston, but a man sleeping on the fourth floor rode his bed to the ground as the building collapsed and walked away.

13. Avoid contemporary **slang** in literary criticism or academic essays. Since slang changes as new words and phrases catch on and unimaginative people mimic them until they get sick of hearing them and adopt new ones, it's useless to give lasting examples here. Try to make the writer's voice seem ageless.

14. Avoid **diction shifts:** Similar to number 13 is the error often marked "diction shift" on student work. Diction refers to the different ways the same idea can be expressed. The variety of word choice in the English language allows us to communicate an idea several ways. "Shut the door," and "Would you be kind enough to close the door, please?" demonstrate two styles of diction, each appropriate in a different situation. A colloquial expression is one more suited to familiar conversation rather than formal writing. In an academic paper about a piece of literature, it is not appropriate to use colloquialisms. The underlined words in the following sentences indicate colloquialisms and are therefore shifts in diction:

> Chaucer was an insightful man who <u>was into</u> religion.

> Thoreau was <u>up front</u> with people and told them openly what he thought.

> During his interview for the journal article, Hemingway <u>came across as</u> as having a <u>macho</u> personality.

> I was <u>really blown away</u> when Hester and Dimmesdale kissed in the forest.

15. Use proper **essay diction** which is more formal than speech. Do not make direct declarations about what an author means. Avoid using the following phrases:

> The author is/was trying to say…
> What the author was trying to say is that…
> What this means (he meant) is that…
> The author meant/means…
> The hidden meaning is…
> The moral of the story is…

Instead, these alternative phrases will keep your essay textbased and produce a more desirable academic tone:

> The text suggests/indicates…
> As the text illustrates,…
> The frequent appearance of _____ in the text suggests…
> The outcome of the novel asserts that…
> The line expresses the poet's concept of…

Overuse of the word "text" can be avoided by referring to it as "the work" or by naming its genre (sonnet, play, poem, epic, novel) but be careful to do it correctly. Don't call just any story a novel.

16. Avoid strained **euphemisms.** A euphemism is the substitution of a mild, indirect or vague expression for a blunt one. Attempts to color or elevate a term by a strained substitution are often awkward and call attention to themselves.

direct term:	euphemism:
criticize	did not like
to die	to pass on, to pass away
slum	inner city housing
committee	special task force
library	communications resource center
gambler	speculator
tax raise	revenue enhancement

State it as it is. Don't cover truth.

17. Avoid **excessive praise** of an author. You will not get a better grade by outlandish claims of your affection for a book or poem. It will only make your instructor suspicious of your sincerity. Besides, essay questions rarely ask for your evaluation of an author because teachers don't want to hear pandering, phoney or unsupported praise. They usually want analysis instead.

18. **Tighten.** Condensing will refine your thinking and clarify and elevate your writing. Tight writing is vigorous, bold, convincing. Section VIII covers tightening more thoroughly.

SECTION X.

CLICHES

Using common or expected word packages or cliches makes your writing unimaginative and your language uninteresting. Trite sayings may once have been apt, but overuse has made them bland. Play with such expressions to make them more original. Instead of using "The horse was as slow as molasses in January," use "gluefooted." Instead of "sadder but wiser," use "taught by sorrow."

Here is a partial list of cliches to avoid:

be there for you

to sum it all up

last but not least

over the hill

without further ado

Live life to its fullest.

beat around the bush

Today is the first day of the rest of your life.

home sweet home

ray of hope

turn the tables

a ton of bricks

safe and sound

share and share alike

as old as the hills

by all means

trials and tribulations

tricks of the trade

for love or money

best foot forward

slow but sure

Better late than never.

play it by ear

Where there's a will there's a way.

pick and choose

ways and means

Give it the old college try.

stick in the mud

Every cloud has a silver lining.
If you've seen one, you've seen them all.
like father, like son
All's fair in love and war
Ignorance is bliss.
Still waters run deep.
You can't teach an old dog new tricks.
Flattery will get you no where.
straight as an arrow
a mountain out of a mole hill
cream of the crop
a drop in a bucket
on pins and needles
as light as a feather
seeing is believing
That's the way the ball bounces.
blind as a bat
dead as a doornail
Two heads are better than one.
bigger and better things
burn your bridges behind you
rise and shine
time and time again
food for thought
knee high to a grasshopper
to wrap it all up
to make matters worse
easier said than done
read between the lines
dog eat dog world
Don't cry over spilled milk.
turn the tables
most prized possession
the world around us
the world in which we live
hard work paid off
more than life itself
wrap things up

PART TWO: GRAMMAR AND USAGE
SECTION XI.

USAGE

Simply put, usage errors refer to a word used incorrectly. This often happens when two words sound alike or nearly alike, or when they are so often misused in everyday speech that, as children, we learn their meaning or application incorrectly, and constant hearing reinforces the mistake. Consult this alphabetical list in editing your work. Become conscious of those words that give you difficulty, and refer to this list when you need to use one of your troublesome words.

a lot	These are two words. They are never united into one. The use of *a lot* is informal style. Instead, use "many" or "a great deal."
accept/except	Accept: verb meaning "to regard as true or valid; to receive something offered; to admit." He accepted my apology. I was accepted by the university of my choice. Except: preposition meaning "excluding." They all went except me.
advice/advise	Advice: noun meaning "assistance or counseling." He always gives me good advice. Advise: verb meaning "to counsel, to suggest a course of action." He advised me to take an earlier flight.
affect/effect	Affect: verb meaning "to influence." The movie affected her and she wept. Effect: noun meaning "the result of something." The effect of the low number of ticket sales was that the dance was canceled. Effect: verb meaning "to accomplish, to bring about a result." Often used in business writing but rarely used in student compositions. The board of directors effected a solution.
already	Means "at this time." It is already done. It is done now.

all ready	Means "all of them are ready." Are you all ready to go? (all of you) Are you all ready to go? (completely ready)
all right	This is always two words. Never spell it *alright*.
among/between	Use *among* for three or more. Use *between* for two. The money was divided among the four players. The two brothers divided the money between themselves.
because	This word can start a sentence, but when it does, it sometimes results in a sentence fragment. *Because* is a conjunction and is used to join two sentences (two independent clauses). He didn't do it because he was too tired. If you start with *because*, you must include both independent clauses: **CORRECT:** Because he was tired, he didn't go. Note: If you start with *because* and only give one clause, it's a fragment. **INCORRECT:** Because he was tired.
cause	Often students use this as a shortened form of *because*. As a slang form, *'cause* is acceptable only when writing dialogue in a story or play if preceded by an apostrophe. Never use it in an essay.
could of	*Could of, might of, should of, would of* are all mistakes which occur from mis-hearing slurred speech. When we contract (join) *could have* to *could've*, it might sound like *could of*. It is never right. Always use *could have* or the contraction.
each and every	Always avoid. Simply use "every"
effect	See "affect."
etc.	Avoid. In academic writing, an item important enough to call for *etc.* is important enough to name. In an essay it is often a misguided attempt to imply that you know more than you have indicated but space is too limited to include it. If there is more to say, say it.
except	See *accept*.
farther/further	Farther: Only used when speaking of distance. Rome is farther from London than Paris is. Further: Can be used for distance, but more commonly used to indicate "to a greater extent," or "to an advanced degree." You will go further in life if you learn to write well.

firstly, secondly	Avoid. Use *first, second.*
good/well	*Good* is an adjective used to describe a noun (person, place, thing or idea). It is a good idea. It's a good place to go for pizza. *Well* is an adverb used to describe an action (verb). **CORRECT:** She sings well enough to be in opera. **INCORRECT:** She sings good enough to be in opera. *Well* can also be used to modify another adjective. He is well liked throughout the county.
hopefully	*Hopefully* modifies a verb. That is, it says how an action is done; in what manner it is accomplished. It cannot be used to indicate the frame of mind or the wishes of the doer of the action. **INCORRECT:** In this letter, you will find the information you requested. Hopefully it will arrive on time. (Incorrect because the information is not arriving in a hopeful manner. The sender is hopeful.) **INCORRECT:** Hopefully she will figure out what I meant. (Incorrect because she isn't figuring out the meaning in a hopeful way.) **INCORRECT:** He just picked someone's number. Hopefully it's mine. **INCORRECT:** Hopefully she won't get angry at us. **CORRECT:** I hope she won't get angry… The adverb *hopefully* must modify the verb. It must describe how the action is enacted. **CORRECT:** He wrote the letter hopefully. (He wrote the letter with hope in his heart and that showed in his manner of writing.) **CORRECT:** Hopefully she walked up to the personnel officer's desk and handed him her application with a smile. (Her manner of walking and presenting the application was hopeful.)
imply/infer	Imply: "to indicate or suggest." The letter implies that his actions are immoral. Infer: "to conclude or judge from some evidence." I inferred from the letter that his actions were immoral. Did you infer that we were supposed to do it today?
irregardless	Should be "regardless."

its/it's	Its: possessive of "it." Roman society and its literature are studied in Latin class. The bird lost its wing. It's: contraction of "it is." It's too late. It's going to be easy.
lie	to tell a lie Present: He lies to me frequently. He is lying now. Past: He lied to me yesterday. Past perfect: He has lied to me many times
lie	to recline, to put one's body in a horizontal position. Note: Use this word when there's no object, when you are doing the action with your whole body. Present: I lie out in the sun every afternoon. Past: Yesterday I lay out in the sun until 3:00. Past perfect: I have often lain on this beach.
lay	to put or place something down Note: Use this word when there is an object, when you're doing the action to something else. Present: I always lay my books down in the hallway. Past: I laid my head on the pillow and immediately fell asleep. Past perfect: I have laid my pen somewhere and now I can't find it.
like when	Never use these two words together. They are always ungrammatical and there are better ways to introduce an example. POOR: Hemingway writes good dialogue. Like when Frederick is talking to Rinaldi about war medals. BETTER: Hemingway writes good dialogue. A fine example is when Frederick is talking to Rinaldi about war medals.
might of/must of	Never correct. See "could of" for explanation.
moral/morale	As a noun, *moral* is a personal principle of behavior, a statement in a code of ethics. Example as noun: His morals are high. As an adjective, *moral* conveys the idea that the person follows a sound code of ethics. Example as adjective: He is a moral individual.

Morale, a noun, refers to the spirit or frame of mind of a group of people.
After getting a raise, the staff morale was high.

past/passed   Past: adverb indicating a location or time.
Don't drive past my street.
It's half past one.

Passed: past tense of the verb "to pass."
I passed the test.
I passed your street.

principal   Adjective: the main part of something.
The principal reason for the decision
The principal ingredient in the recipe
The principal or the headmaster of a school

principle   Noun: an ethic or rule of conduct, a moral guideline.
His principles forbid the telling of lies.

Also, more generally any rule, especially in science.
The principles of geometry…

should of   Never correct. See "could of" for explanation.

since   Refers to time, not cause. Do not use *since* instead of *because* when you wish to indicate cause.

than/then   Than: used in comparisons.
He is shorter than I am.

Then: Adverb. Use when indicating the relationship in time of two events.
She went home first. Then she called him.

than   Any sentence using "than" should be examined to see if missing words cause ambiguity.

POOR: I am closer to my mother than my father. (Does this mean that my father is less close to my mother than I am? The writer could have meant that he is closer to his mother than he is to his father. Extend the sentence to clarify.)

BETTER: I am closer to my mother than to my father.

ALSO CLEAR: I am closer to my mother than my father is.

their   Pronoun: belonging to them.
It is their family business.

there	Adverb used to imply a location. I think it's over there.
	Adverb used to introduce a sentence. There is a stop sign on the corner. There are two sisters in the family. (Choose *is* or *are* depending on whether the noun following the verb is singular or plural.)
they're	Contraction of "they are." They're going to New England in the fall.
to/too	To: preposition indicating direction. He went to school. Give it to me.
	Too: adverb used before an adjective. It is too bad she's can't spell. They were too late to catch the bus. It is too hot to work.
	Memory device: When you mean an excessive amount of something (heat, cold), then use an excessive amount of "o's."
try to	**INCORRECT:** I am going to try <u>and</u> earn better grades. **CORRECT:** I am going to try <u>to</u> earn better grades.
very	Avoid. Where emphasis is necessary, use words that are strong in themselves.
	POOR: She is a very nice woman. **BETTER:** She is kind, sociable and even-tempered.
	POOR: It was very hot yesterday. **BETTER:** It was scorching yesterday.
who/whom	Who: Use in questions asking the identity of someone. Who told you that? Who is that man?
	Also, use in sentences that elaborate on the subject expressed at the beginning of the sentence. In such cases, the word following "who" will be a verb. Lincoln was the president who signed the Emancipation Proclamation.
	Whom: Use in sentences where the word following it is another noun or pronoun, not a verb. **INCORRECT:** He is the man who I told you about. **CORRECT:** He is the man whom I told you about. After *whom* there is another subject, in this case, the pronoun "I."

who's/whose	Who's: contraction of who is or who has. Who's going to do it? Who's got my book? (Colloquial for "Who has my book?") Whose: Use to indicate possessive, or when you can't separate into "who is" or "who has." Whose jacket is this? I don't know whose book this is. Robert Frost's poem begins, "Whose woods these are I think I know."
would of	Never correct. See "could of" for explanation.
your/you're	Your: possessive of "you." It's your book. Your writing is improving. You're: contraction of "you are." You're improving every day.

SECTION XII.

USE OF APOSTROPHE

Use an apostrophe in these cases:

1. Nouns form the possessive by adding an apostrophe and an "s."

>   a man's hat
>   Milton's poems
>   men's hats
>   children's books

So do indefinite pronouns (such as "one" when referring to a person).

>   one's self-respect
>   everyone's family

Note that the first noun doesn't have to be a person:

>   society's problems
>   the room's atmosphere
>   a nation's leaders

2. Plural nouns which end in "s" form the possessive by adding an apostrophe only.

>   the boys' bicycles
>   a girls' school
>   the waitresses' uniforms
>   ladies' clothes
>   the Joneses' house

(The name Jones is used as plural and possessive here. It indicates the house that belongs to both of the Joneses.)

3. Singular nouns which end in "s" form the possessive by adding an apostrophe and an "s" if the "s" is pronounced as an extra syllable.

>   Keats's poems
>   Mr. Thomas's house
>   a waitress's uniform

4. However, if an extra syllable would be awkward to pronounce, the possessive is formed by adding the apostrophe only and omitting the second "s."

>   Ulysses' voyages
>   Moses' life

Euripides' plays
Jesus' teachings

5. Use an apostrophe to indicate omitted letters in contracted words and dates.

haven't, doesn't, isn't, it's
o'clock, o'er
the class of '53
the hurricane of '38

6. "It's" means "it is". Use an apostrophe **ONLY** if your sentence using "it's" can be stretched out to "it is".

It's not my fault that I can never use apostrophes correctly. (That is, "It is not my fault...")

Its without an apostrophe is the possessive of "it."

Examples:

Society and its problems are always changing.
The report is well written. Its significance is clear.
The table is old. One of its legs is broken.

Do NOT use an apostrophe in these cases:

1. Plurals that are not possessives:

INCORRECT: Three girl's were talking.
CORRECT: Three girls were talking.

2. Verbs that end in "s"

INCORRECT: He sit's under the tree.
CORRECT: He sits under the tree.

INCORRECT: He always think's too much.
CORRECT: He always thinks too much.

3. Possessive pronouns that end in "s"

INCORRECT: your's, our's
CORRECT: yours, ours

INCORRECT: it's (when referring to something owned or belonging to or part of "it")

SECTION XIII.

OTHER PUNCTUATION RULES

A. Use of Colon

1. The principal use of the colon is to introduce a formal list, a long quotation, or an explanatory statement.

> There were three causes of the rebellion: inadequate housing, injustice, and starvation.

> In 1803 Thomas Jefferson said: "We have seen with sincere concern the flames of war lighted up again in Europe...."
> (A long quotation follows.)

> The excessive materialism and lack of meaningful values in the 1920's reminded Gertrude Stein of a remark she heard a gas station attendant say: "We are all a lost generation."

> Huck regarded the need for table manners as an uncivilized individual might: as an incomprehensible nuisance.

Note that the sentence preceding the colon should be grammatically complete without the list.

> **INCORRECT:** We furnish: towels, sheets, pillow slips, dishes, cooking utensils, silverware.

> **CORRECT:** We furnish all you will need: towels, sheets....

2. The colon may be used between two principal clauses when the second clause explains or develops the first.

> The editorial argued that there is one strong reason why gambling should not be legalized: gambling establishments tend to attract undesirable individuals.

3. A colon is used after a formal salutation in a business letter.
> Dear Madam:
> Gentlemen:
> Dear Mrs. Harris:

B. Use of Semicolon

1. A semicolon is used to mark a more important break in the sentence flow than that marked by a comma, as follows:

> John Steinbeck wrote novels which took place in the American West; however, that was not the West of prairies and range wars, but of life in small California agricultural towns and along the coast.

As illustrated above, a semicolon is required to separate two independent clauses (what appears to be two separate sentences, each with a subject and verb): In this case it functions like a period when the two sentences are closely related.

> I do not say that these stories are untrue; I only say I do not believe them.

> **Run-on sentence:** I had hoped to find a summer job at the resort, however, two weeks of job-hunting convinced me that it was impossible.

> **Correct:** I had hoped to find a summer job at the resort; however, two weeks of job-hunting convinced me that it was impossible.

2. Even when two independent clauses (two sentences) are joined by a conjunction (such as *and, or, but, because, although*), a semicolon **may** be used to separate them if the clauses are particularly long or are subdivided by commas. The purpose of the semicolon in such a sentence is to make the break between the two clauses greater than the breaks within the clauses.

> The male protagonist of Hawthorne's novel, Arthur Dimmesdale, a Puritan minister, was actually a sinner, at least according to the doctrine he preached; but the town, so captivated by the spiritual devoutness and humility of his sermons, never suspected him.

Note: The reason for using the semicolon is the presence of so many other commas and the length and complexity of the sentence. In shorter sentences it's not necessary to use a semicolon before the conjunction *but*. A comma will suffice.

3. A semicolon is used to separate elements in a series when the elements contain internal commas. That is, when a comma is not a strong enough mark of separation to indicate the elements of a series unmistakably, a semicolon is used instead.

> **Ambiguous:** The committee consisted of Mr. Webster, the president of the bank, Mr. Elton, the manager of the water company, and the mayor. (How many people were on the committee?)

> **Correct:** The committee consisted of Mr. Webster, the president of the bank; Mr. Elton, the manager of the water company; and the Mayor. (Here there are clearly three men on the committee.)

C. Use of Quotation Marks

1. Use quotation marks to enclose a direct quotation, but not an indirect quotation. A direct quotation gives the exact words of a speaker. An indirect quotation is the writer's paraphrase of what someone said.

> **INCORRECT:** He said "that he was sorry." (This is an indirect quotation since it does not give his exact words.)
>
> **CORRECT:** He said that he was sorry.
>
> **CORRECT:** He said, "I'm sorry." (Since this gives his exact words, it is a direct quotation.)

2. If a quotation consists of several sentences, uninterrupted by a *he-said* expression, use one set of marks to enclose the entire quotation. Do not enclose each separate sentence. If a quotation consists of several paragraphs, put quotation marks at the beginning of each paragraph but only at the end of the last paragraph.

3. Quotation marks are used for material directly quoted from another writer, but not for a paraphrase (a rewording) of an author's ideas.

4. When a quotation is four or more lines of print, it is set off by indenting each line at the right and left, and by single-spacing. Do not use quotation marks when the quoted material is indented. Then your double spaced paper should look like this:

> Milton ends the last book of *Paradise Lost*, his epic poem about the fall of Adam
>
> and Eve, with these famous lines:
>
>> The world was all before them, where to choose Their place of rest, and Providence their guide. They hand in hand with wandering steps and slow, Through Eden took their solitary way.

5. A question mark or exclamation mark goes inside the quotation mark if it applies to the quotation only, and outside the quotation mark if it applies to the whole sentence.

> My father said, "Are you hurt?"
> "Where's the light switch?" Her voice sounded fearful.
> The captain said, "God help us!"

But:

> Did the minister end the funeral service by saying, "Rest in peace"?

6. Titles of books, full-length plays (three to five acts), epic poems published as the entire text of a volume, magazines and newspapers should not have quotation marks, but should be underlined or put in italics. Titles of poems, one-act plays, short stories, articles, songs (i.e. shorter selections printed within a volume of a different title) carry quotation marks.

> *Hamlet* or <u>Hamlet</u>
> *New York Times* or <u>New York Times</u>
> *The Scarlet Letter* or <u>The Scarlet Letter</u>
> "Rime of the Ancient Mariner"
> "Birches"
> "On the Duty of Civil Disobedience"

7. For a quote within a quote, surround single quotation marks by double ones.

> In Thoreau's essay "On the Duty of Civil Disobedience," he says, "I heartily accept the motto 'that government is best which governs least.'"

D. Use of Dash

1. Dashes may be used to set off an appositive, which is a phrase or group of words that renames a noun or clarifies it. The sentence would make sense without the appositive but it would not be as clear.

> Mr. Jones—the only man who witnessed the murder—was absent at the trial.

> Three ships—a yawl, a sloop, and a schooner—were anchored in the harbor.

(If the commas were used to set off "a yawl, a sloop, and a schooner," the sentence might be misunderstood to refer to six ships. The dashes make it clear that only three ships are meant.)

Note that the dash is made on the keyboard with two hyphens and no spaces before or after.

2. Dashes may be used to set off parenthetic elements when commas are not strong enough.

> By the time the speech was over—it lasted almost two hours—I was dozing in my chair.

(Since the parenthetic element is an independent clause and could stand by itself as a sentence, commas would be insufficient to set it off clearly.)

> Martin Luther's criticisms of the Church—the sale of pardons and indulgences, high clerical officials living in excessive luxury, elaborate and costly ornamentation of churches, and the susceptibility of clerics to corruption—were not all resolved with the Protestant Reformation.

(Because the list between dashes is so detailed and contains commas within it, commas surrounding it would not be strong enough to set it off.)

SECTION XIV.

AGREEMENT ERRORS

In grammar, the word "agreement" means likeness. To make two words agree is to make them alike in some respect, usually matching singular words with singular, and plural with plural.

Here are the rules:

1. A singular verb is used with a singular subject. A plural verb is used with a plural subject.

> The book (singular) **opens** easily.
> The books (plural) **open** easily.

Note that if there is an "s" on the subject to indicate plural, there is no "s" on the verb, and vice versa.

2. The verb agrees only with its subject. Occasionally a word (perhaps a noun in a prepositional phrase) occurs between the subject and the verb. This word has no effect upon whether the verb is singular or plural, even though it is closer to the verb than the subject is.

> The truck, loaded with boxes of apples, **is** speeding.
> (*Truck* is the subject, not *boxes* or *apples*.)

> One of the photos **shows** our camp.
> (*One* is the subject, not *photos*.)

> The old maps of the country **show** the coastlines accurately.
> (*Maps* is the subject, not *country*.)

Parenthetical remarks or phrases within dashes should not be matched with the verb.

INCORRECT: The problems of adolescence—the trials and conflicts with an older generation, the adventure of falling in love, the challenge of peer pressure—provides good subject matter for stories.

CORRECT: The problems of adolescence—the trials and conflicts with an older generation, the adventure of falling in love, the challenge of peer pressure—provide good subject matter for stories.

Problems is the subject, so it must be *problems provide*.

3. A singular subject remains singular even if other nouns are connected to it by words such as *with, as well as, in addition to, except, together with*, and *no less than*.

His sense of humor as well as his language **is** not refined.
  (*Sense* is the subject.)

The doctor, together with the nurses, **was** working feverishly.
  (*Doctor* is the subject.)

Your voice, as well as your walk, **gives** you away.
  (*Voice* is the subject.)

The knights, no less than King Arthur, **are** to be honored.
  (*Knights* is the subject.)

4. Some indefinite pronouns are always singular. Others are always plural. Some may be either singular or plural.

Singular			Plural
each	everyone	anyone	several
either	everybody	someone	few
neither	no one	somebody	both
one	nobody		many

Each of the cars **has** a mechanical problem.

Neither of the coaches **wants** to complain.

Everybody in the stands **was** excited.

But:

Several in this box **are** spoiled.

Few of the students at this school **are** lazy.

Note that with these troublesome singular pronouns that sound like plural ones (*everyone, anyone, someone*, etc), all other pronouns in the rest of the sentence referring to them must also be singular.

  Someone forgot **his** lunch.

It is incorrect to use *their* instead of *his* simply because the gender of the lunch owner is unknown. See Section XVII, Common Grammatical Errors, Part 1, for a more thorough explanation of this important concept.

5. Some pronouns are singular or plural, depending on the situation. *Some, all, most, none,* and *any* are singular when they refer to a quantity or amount of something that cannot be divided into parts. They are plural when they refer to a number of things that can be counted.

Some of the milk **was** spoiled.	**(quantity)**
Some of the tickets **were** returned.	**(number)**

54

Most of the music **is** easy enough. (quantity)
Most of the players **like** the coach. (number)

All of the pie **was** eaten. (quantity)
All of the pictures **were** lost. (number)

6. Singular words joined by *or, nor, either-or, neither-nor* are singular.

Neither your manner nor your argument is convincing.
Either Jim or Bill has your jacket.
Dad or Mom drives us to school.
(It's one or the other—Dad or Mom—not both, so the verb is singular.)

Note that in the above examples, each of the pair of subjects (manner, Jim, Mom, etc.) is singular. But when a singular subject and a plural subject are joined by *or* or *nor*, the verb agrees with the subject that is nearer to it.

Neither the firemen nor the fire **chief knows** how the fire started.
Neither the fire chief nor the **firemen know** how the fire started.

Either the first paragraph or the last two **paragraphs are** unnecessary.
Either the last two paragraphs or the first **paragraph is** unnecessary.

7. Sometimes the verb precedes the subject in a sentence. The speaker must think ahead to the subject in order to decide whether the verb is to be singular or plural.

INCORRECT: Here's the **skis** for Dave.
CORRECT: Here are the **skis** for Dave.

INCORRECT: There's three **reasons** why I can't go.
CORRECT: There are three **reasons** why I can't go.

8. When an "ing" verb serves as the subject of the sentence, it is singular.

Skiing is my favorite sport.

The problem is apt to occur when there are other words between the "ing" verb used as a subject and the main verb in the sentence.

INCORRECT: Asking myself these questions have helped me to set personal and academic goals.
CORRECT: Asking myself these questions has helped me....

SECTION XV.

HOW TO FIND FRAGMENTS

A sentence fragment is an incomplete sentence, missing one of its basic parts, often a subject and verb. Sentence fragments also occur when a sentence is linked by a conjunction to another sentence, but that second sentence isn't attached.

To understand this explanation, you must know these terms:

Subject: The "do-er" of the action in the sentence. It could be a person; it could be a thing.

Verb: The action done in a sentence or the word that conveys that something exists.

Complement: The word or group of words that completes the action in a sentence. In these examples, the underlined portion is a complement:

He went to the beach.
She walked lazily through the room.
The teacher understood the students' dilemma.
He wrote angry criticisms of social conditions.

Conjunction: A word used to join parts of a sentence. Examples: *because, since, that, after, although, before, and, or.* For a complete list, see Section XVIII, Parts of Speech.

Independent clause: Another term for a correct sentence because it has subject, verb and usually a complement. An independent clause can stand by itself as a sentence, and is represented by the sentence pattern, **SVC** (subject, verb, complement).

Example:

Twain's main character is Huckleberry.

Subject: Twain's main character
Verb: is
Complement: Huckleberry

Dependent clause: A subject and a verb preceded by a conjunction which links it to a previous complete sentence. It is represented by the sentence pattern, **conj SVC**. It is not a complete or correct sentence.

Example:

Because Twain's main character is Huck Finn

Conjunction: because

Types of fragments:

1. One common kind of fragment is a dependent clause floating by itself. It looks like this: **conj SVC**. You may need to memorize the list of conjunctions (see Section XVIII, Parts of Speech) to be able to recognize this pattern. Often it appears as a mistake in your writing, like this: **SVC. conj SVC**. The error that makes this incorrect is the period after the first SVC. It should be eliminated or changed to a comma.

> **INCORRECT:** One of the nation's fastest growing forms of recreation is whitewater rafting. Which I like to do often.

The word *which* is a conjunction that should be used to join the two clauses.

Some answers to why-questions are given as fragments when the speaker or writer does not repeat the question in his answer but just starts with *because*.

Example:

> Why did Chillingworth wither away and die after Dimmesdale died on the scaffold? Because he had no more purpose in life.

The answer is a sentence fragment because it is a dependent clause. It is only the last half of the complete idea. The conjunction fragment (**conj SVC**) must be linked to an independent clause (another sentence).

> **CORRECT:** He died because he had no more purpose in life.
> **ALSO CORRECT:** Why did Chillingworth die? He had no more purpose in life.

The reason for the error in the incorrect version is the conjunction *because* at the beginning of the sentence. Without it, the sentence is correct.

If a sentence has a dependent clause it must also have an independent clause. The dependent clause (**conj SVC**) can appear first, before the independent clause, if it is hooked by a comma. Then it looks like this: **conj SVC, SVC**.

> Since it's three o'clock already, I think I'll go home.
> Conjunction: since

If a period were there instead of a comma, it would be incorrect.

> **INCORRECT:** Since it's three o'clock already. I think I'll go home.
> **INCORRECT:** Although rafting is the nation's fastest growing recreation. I don't like it.
> **INCORRECT:** Because Emily Dickinson used unconventional spelling in her poems. Many critics considered her an amateur.

All of these are incorrect because the first dependent clauses in each sentence (**conj SVC**) are detached and they shouldn't be. When you use the reverse pattern to join two clauses, putting the dependent clause first, then you must put a comma between them.

CORRECT: Although rafting is the nation's fastest growing recreation, I don't like it.

CORRECT: Because Emily Dickinson used unconventional spelling in her poems, many critics considered her an amateur.

2. Another kind of fragment error results when you use the word *that*. Be careful every time you use this word. *That* can be a pronoun (for example: That is wrong), or an adjective (for example: That man is handsome) or a conjunction (for example: I didn't know that you knew him).

The problem comes when you use the word *that* as a conjunction and you stop the sentence just before it. This tends to happen in two cases:

A. In a series of "**that SVC**" patterns with one or more such patterns detached from the beginning of the sentence.

INCORRECT: I need to remember that I have obligations at home. And that I can't indulge all my whims.

Note that it makes no difference whether the second clause beginning with "that" is preceded by "and." It's still wrong because it's a dependent clause, dependent on being attached to the first clause by *and* as well as by *that*.

B. An answer to a question is often preceded with the word *that* which makes it a dependent clause.

INCORRECT: What did Hamlet learn from the ghost?
That his uncle killed his father in the orchard.

The answer is a dependent clause fragment. It should read: "He learned that his uncle…."

3. Some fragments are detached appositives, phrases which explain the identity of the complement (i.e. the last noun in the previous, wrongly detached sentence).

INCORRECT: She won first prize. A trip to Hawaii.

INCORRECT: I contacted Mr Jones. The Vice President of General Motors in charge of marketing.

In both cases, these appositives should be attached with a comma. They will not be detected by you as fragments if you read them aloud smoothly after the previous sentence. They will only stand out as fragments when you read them alone. Therefore, it's important that in your proofreading, you mentally separate every sentence from those around it.

4. Another type of fragment often occurs when you are giving an example to prove something you've just said.

INCORRECT: Hawthorne uses many symbols in *The Scarlet Letter*. For example, the red letter A in the sky and on Hester's dress, the rose by the prison door, and the scaffold.

The second sentence is a fragment because it's only a list preceded by the prepositional phrase "for example." There's no subject and no verb in the sentence. Instead, introduce the list this way: "Good examples are the red letter...." Now you have a subject (*examples*) and a verb (*are*).

Even if you had only one example instead of a list, putting it by itself after the "for example" would still have been wrong because it wouldn't have a subject and verb of its own.

Only use "for example" if what follows is a complete sentence.

INCORRECT: Hawthorne uses many symbols in *The Scarlet Letter*. For example, the letter A.

CORRECT: Hawthorne uses many symbols in *The Scarlet Letter*. For example, the letter A stands for adultery.

How to find fragments:

Proofread by separating each sentence from the one before it and the one after it. Do not link them together in your mind. Read each one twice in order to separate it from the previous sentence. You may even need to read your essay sentence-by-sentence backwards in order to separate effectively. In other words, read the last sentence of your essay all by itself. Even read it twice. Then read the one that is next to the last, etc. This will make them stand out separately. Reading them in the right order lulls you into thinking that they are all right because they "sound good."

SECTION XVI.

RUN-ON SENTENCES

Though run-on sentences are common errors, they are easily corrected if you understand the six terms explained at the beginning of Section XV, "Sentence Fragments." Review them before proceeding.

A run-on error, often called a comma fault or comma splice, occurs whenever two sentences are run together when they should be separated. The division is often marked by a comma, but a comma is insufficient punctuation.

Here's how to look for them:

1. Don't just look for overly long sentences. Run-ons can be short, too.

   INCORRECT: He stumbled, then he fell.

Every time you use a new subject (like "he" in the example) and a new verb (like "fell"), you might be starting a new sentence unless it's linked together with a conjunction (See Section XVIII, "Parts of Speech," for a list of conjunctions. "Then" is not a conjunction.)

2. Look for these **incorrect** sentence patterns:

   SV, SV
   SVC, SVC
   SV, SVC
   SVC, SV

Note: S = subject, V = verb, C = complement. See previous section for definitions.

In other words, a comma cannot join two independent clauses (sentences). Whether or not each independent clause (sentence) has a complement is irrelevant here. Even if the two sentences are related in meaning, or if there is a cause and effect or a sequential relationship, the two sentences must not be joined by a comma alone.

3. Examine each comma you have used in your writing. Consider what precedes it and what follows it to determine whether both parts can stand by themselves as separate sentences (independent clauses). If they both can, and you have joined them by a comma without a conjunction, then you have a run-on.

There are three ways to correct run-ons:

   a. Use a semi-colon between the two sentences.
   b. Join the two sentences with a conjunction (*and, but, or, although, because, while, as if, unless*, etc. See Section XVIII, part 8, pp. 71-72).

c. Divide them into two separate sentences using a period.

Beware:

Some words seem like conjunctions but aren't. (Study Part 8 of Section XVIII, Parts of Speech, to find them.) *Then, however* and *therefore* are commonly misused to join two sentences but they are not conjunctions. They cannot correctly join two sentences. This frequent error can easily be corrected.

INCORRECT: I would like to help you out, however I don't think I'll have time.
CORRECT: I would like to help you out; however, I don't think I'll have time.

(You may also divide these correct versions into two separate sentences.)

INCORRECT: Our government needs more revenue, therefore we need to raise taxes.
CORRECT: Our government needs more revenue; therefore, we need to raise taxes.

INCORRECT: The lookout man spotted a small whiff of smoke, then he called the park headquarters.
CORRECT: The lookout man spotted a small whiff of smoke. Then he called....

SECTION XVII.

COMMON GRAMMATICAL ERRORS

1. PRONOUN-ANTECEDENT AGREEMENT:

All pronouns used in a sentence must agree in number with the nouns to which they refer (called the antecedent or referent). If the antecedent is singular, then all the pronouns which refer to that antecedent must be singular. If the antecedent is plural, then the pronoun referring to it must be plural.

CORRECT: People who pay income tax must file their forms by April 15.

Subject: People (plural)
Antecedent: their (plural pronoun which refers to people)

CORRECT: All of my friends forgot their books.

INCORRECT: Everyone forgot their books.

CORRECT: Everyone forgot his book.

The reason for the incorrect sentence using "everyone" as the subject is that "everyone" is a singular pronoun. It's an odd quirk in the language, but note the last syllable, "one." The same is true for "everybody."

Many pronouns that seem like they should be plural are actually singular. Here are some examples:

everyone	everybody
someone	somebody
no one	nobody
anyone	anybody

All these words are singular, but we make the mistake of using plural pronouns for them.

INCORRECT: Anyone who reads good literature will improve their language usage.

CORRECT: Anyone who reads good literature will improve his language usage.

People make this mistake because *everyone* probably consists of men and women and they don't want to have to choose between the male and female singular pronoun. This is particularly true when the pronoun is an unidentified *someone*. To avoid this, people have shifted incorrectly to the plural until it is so commonly used that it seems right to some people.

This raises a gender issue. Traditional English grammar dictates the use of the male pronoun.

INCORRECT: Anyone who can't remember their schedule should write it down.
CORRECT: Anyone who can't remember his schedule should write it down.

INCORRECT: Someone left their backpack here.

We make this mistake when we don't know if the *someone* is male or female.

CORRECT: Someone left his backpack here.

On legal documents, government publications, and in certain business situations, it is now common to use both the male and female pronoun together, like this:

CORRECT: Everyone who works at a salaried job must file his/her income tax by April 15.

ALSO CORRECT: Everyone who works…must file his or her income tax….

This can become cumbersome, especially if the pronoun is used more than once in the same sentence. Some writers try to avoid this by writing in the passive voice:

Income tax must be filed by April 15 by everyone who works at a salaried job.

Yet many sentences written in passive sound flat and dead. In fact, for most writing, they are not recommended. When you want to avoid bland passive sentences or awkward phrases using both pronouns, choose one gender. Recently, the female is chosen with just as much authority:

Anyone who can adjust her working hours to fill in during the Christmas rush should contact the front office today.

2. INCORRECT PRONOUN CASE:

All pronouns fit one of the following cases or categories:

Subject	Object	Possessive
I	me	my, mine
you	you	your, yours
he	him	his, his
she	her	her, hers
we	us	our, ours
they	them	their, theirs

Usually people have no difficulty using possessive pronouns. The problem arises when they mix object and subject pronouns.

Subject pronouns are used for the "do-er" of the action in a sentence, that is, the subject. Subject pronouns precede the verb.

> He felt lost.
> She walked outside.
> Mary and I went home.

He, she and *I* are all subject pronouns.

Object pronouns are used when the person is a receiver of the action. They follow the verb.

> His boss paid him.   (He received the money.)
> The king executed her.   (She received the axe.)

Him and *her* are object pronouns.

Object pronouns are also used following a preposition, as in a prepositional phrase. Often the whole prepositional phrase follows a verb.

> Father gave $5.50 to each of them. (*Of* is a preposition.)
> The gift was addressed to me. (*To* is a preposition.)

Them and *me* are object pronouns.

Both of the above examples are correct. The problem arises when two pronouns are used together. When a small child asks his mother, "Can me and Johnny go out to play?" the mother cringes and corrects, "Can Johnny and I go out to play." Her correction is sound, but only when the pronouns in question are subject pronouns. When the pronouns are object pronouns, "Johnny and me" is correct, as in "Give some to Johnny and me." However, parents who have learned to change "Johnny and me" to "Johnny and I" sometimes correct what's already correct. They fly into a fit upon hearing "Johnny and me" and mistakenly think that it's always wrong or that "Johnny and I" has a more elegant sound. The result is that children never learn to make a distinction between pronouns that precede and those that follow the verb.

> **INCORRECT:** The gift was addressed to John and I.
> **EQUALLY INCORRECT:** The gift was addressed to John and myself.
> **CORRECT:** The gift was addressed to John and me.
>
> **INCORRECT:** He tripped over George and I as he walked down the aisle.
>
> **INCORRECT:** Minutes of the last meeting were sent to the committee and I.
>
> **INCORRECT:** The society misjudged Arthur and she.
>
> **INCORRECT:** I have forgotten Grandmother and he.
>
> **INCORRECT:** Scholarships were given to Robert, Jennifer and I.

There's an easy way to correct this problem: Temporarily remove the first object pronoun of the pair and see how that sounds. Your ear is a more accurate judge than you might think. You would never say "The minutes were sent to I," or "The society misjudged

64

she," or "A scholarship was given to I." It sounds terrible! Just because there is another person between the verb and the pronoun in question does not change the pronoun from the object case to the subject case. You would naturally say "The minutes were sent to me." Now just insert the other object.

Another problem occurs when people think they are speaking elegantly by using the "I" form after the preposition "between."

INCORRECT: Just between you and I, darling, I think they're a terrible match.

(*Between* is a preposition. Pronouns following a preposition must be object pronouns.)

CORRECT: Just between you and me,…

3. DANGLING MODIFIER:

A modifier is a word or a group of words which describe another word in the sentence. Such a modifying group of words preceding the subject of a sentence must modify that subject.

CORRECT: An orphan without much education, Huckleberry Finn learned from the people he met along the Mississippi River.

Here, "an orphan without much education" is the modifying phrase.

Occasionally a modifying or descriptive phrase preceding the subject of a sentence causes an error by not modifying the subject. Such misplaced or dangling modifying phrases may be of four types:

1. Participial phrases

2. Appositives

3. Prepositional phrases

4. Adjectives or adjective phrases

A. Participial Phrase Modifiers:

A participial phrase is a group of words containing an *ing*-verb or an *ed*-verb. When it is used to modify some subject, it often begins the sentence and is set off from the rest of the sentence by a comma.

CORRECT: Painted with a fresh coat of clean white, the house looked new again.

CORRECT: Running to catch the bus, I tripped over my own foot.

The phrases beginning with "painted" and "running" are participial phrases.

A participial phrase at the beginning of a sentence must refer to the subject of the sentence. In other words, the thing painted or the person doing the running must be the subject of the main verb in the sentence.

INCORRECT EXAMPLES:

Running to catch the bus, the driver drove off.
(The driver didn't do the running.)

Being a Hawaiian, the photographs were wonderfully exotic.
(The photographs weren't Hawaiian; the photographer or the person photographed was.)

Growing up in a slum, my personality has developed through encounters with undesirable individuals.
(Your personality didn't grow up in a slum; you did.)

INCORRECT: Walking slowly down the road, he saw a woman accompanied by two children.

Who is doing the walking, the woman or the man? It's unclear. By the structure of the sentence, we assume "walking" refers to the subject of the sentence, which is the man. If the writer wishes to make it refer to the woman who is walking down the road, he must rewrite the sentence.

CORRECT: He saw a woman accompanied by two children walking slowly down the road.

Participial phrases preceded by a preposition come under the same rule if they begin a sentence.

INCORRECT: On arriving in London, his friends met him at the airport.
(His friends didn't just arrive in London; he did.)

CORRECT: On arriving in London, he found his friends waiting at the airport.

INCORRECT: After traveling widely throughout Europe, Scotland is still my favorite place.
(Scotland didn't do the traveling; you did.)

CORRECT: After traveling widely throughout Europe, I found that Scotland was still my favorite place.

B. Appositive Modifiers:

An appositive is a noun phrase renaming or identifying another noun, in this case the subject of a sentence. If the appositive does not serve to modify the subject of the sentence, it is an error (the dreaded dangling modifier).

INCORRECT: Long thought to be relatively flat and shaped like huge Frisbees, the scientists have found that some galaxies are actually oblong in shape.
(The scientists are not shaped like Frisbees; galaxies are.)

CORRECT: Long thought to be relatively flat and shaped like huge Frisbees, galaxies actually have a variety of shapes, even oblong.

INCORRECT: A student of proven capability and self-discipline, the committee granted him a scholarship.

CORRECT: A student of proven capability and self-discipline, he was granted a scholarship.

C. Prepositional Phrases:

When a preposition phrase initiating the sentence serves as a modifier, it must refer to the subject of the sentence.

INCORRECT: Without a guide to lead him, the way seemed impossible.
(The way didn't lack a guide; the traveler did.)

CORRECT: Without a guide to lead him, the traveler lost his way.

D. Adjective or Adjective Phrase Modifiers:

If adjectives or adjective phrases begin the sentence, they must also modify the subject of the sentence.

INCORRECT: Rejected and homesick, the city seemed barren and frightening to me.
(The city wasn't rejected and homesick.)

CORRECT: Rejected and homesick, I thought the city was barren and frightening.
Sentences violating these rules are often ridiculous:

Missing some essential parts, I was able to buy the bicycle very cheap.

Hoping to go to sleep, the fire alarm sounded.

As a father of five, his checking account is often depleted.

4. LACK OF PARALLELISM:

When a sentence contains a series of words or phrases, each item in the series should be the same part of speech or start with the same part of speech as every other item. When the initial items in the series are different parts of speech, an awkward lack of parallelism results.

INCORRECT: I like swimming, surfing and to ski.
CORRECT: I like swimming, surfing and skiing.
ALSO CORRECT: I like to swim, surf and ski.

INCORRECT: My career choices have been influenced by talking to my family, by my friends and teachers, and from different parts of the world.

CORRECT: My career choices have been influenced by my family, by my friends and teachers, and by exposure to other parts of the world.

In the incorrect sentence, "talking" is a verb and "by" is a preposition. In the correct version, all items are introduced by "by" followed by a noun.

> **INCORRECT:** Her morals included not lying, being sincere and celibacy.

> **CORRECT:** Her morals included honesty, sincerity and celibacy.

> **INCORRECT:** Hemingway's skills consist of deep sea fishing, safaris, the knowledge of bullfights, writing novels, and boxing.

> **CORRECT:** Hemingway's skills consist of deep sea fishing, hunting on safaris, understanding bullfights, writing novels, and boxing.

> **INCORRECT:** Those years have instilled in me an ability to adapt quickly, tolerance for diversity, and gaining a new geographical perspective.

> **CORRECT:** Those years have instilled in me an ability to adapt quickly, tolerance for diversity, and a new geographical perspective.

> **INCORRECT:** The protagonist's goals consisted of total independence, being responsible for her actions, and to get married.
> **CORRECT:** The protagonist's goals consisted of total independence, responsibility for her actions, and marriage.

Correction of parallelism errors results in smoother sentences.

PARTS OF SPEECH

This section is intended for reference only. In other sections on grammar, parts of speech are referred to in explanations and rules. If you don't understand a rule or explanation because you're unsure of the term used, check here.

All words fall into one of eight categories.

Two types:	**Common**	**Proper**
	city	San Diego
	organization	United Nations
	sister	Nancy

1. **NOUNS**—used to name a person, place, thing, or concept.

Note: Common nouns are not capitalized; proper nouns are capitalized.

Noun endings: ment, tion, ity, ty, sion, ism, hood, ness, logy

Subject	Object	Possessive
he	him	his, his
she	her	her, hers
it	it	its, its
I	me	my, mine
we	us	our, ours
you	you	your, yours
they	them	their, theirs

2. **PRONOUNS**—used to replace or substitute for a noun.

Subject pronouns: used as subjects of sentences (usually near the beginning of a sentence, before the verb)

Object pronouns: used as objects of verbs and prepositions (after verbs and prepositions)

Indefinite pronouns: that, these, this, those, most, many, some, few, one, several, everyone, any, anyone, etc.

3. **ADJECTIVES**—used to describe or modify a noun or pronoun.

Adjective endings: al, able, ible, ous, tious, ful, ive, ic, tic, and others.

Test for adjective: If you don't know whether a word is an adjective, then say the word in question and follow it with any of the following:

> book
> place
> person
> idea

If at least one of the resulting phrases makes sense, then it's an adjective.

4. **VERBS**—used to designate action, being or a condition.

Verb endings: ize, ate

Type A: **Action verb.** This type indicates what is happening even if it is not visual. Examples: run, think, have, consider

Type B. **Being verb.** This type simply tells that something exists. Tenses of the verb "to be" are *is, was, has been, will be*, etc.

Type C: Helping verbs or auxiliary verbs. This type can be used with either Types A or B to indicate a tense. Examples: has, have, had, must, might, should, could, can, would, will. Also the following can be used with "ing" verbs: was, is, are, am, were, etc.

Infinitive: A verb that is not conjugated to accompany a subject and does not indicate a tense. Examples: to run, to facilitate, to think.

5. **ADVERBS**—three types

A. Adverbs modify verbs. They add some information to how or when or where the action of the verb was done.

Test for Type A Adverbs: Say the verb and then ask: Where? How? When? How much? (or to what extent?)

I am going to go **tomorrow**.	When?
She sings **beautifully**.	How?
He **always** knows.	To what extent?
I went **outside**.	Where?
I do **not** like to ski.	How much, or to what extent?

Tomorrow, beautifully, always, outside and *not* are all adverbs.

B. Adverbs modify adjectives. Usually they intensify adjectives.

the dark red dress
   adv adj n

an extremely happy person
     adv   adj   n

I was so tired.
 v adv adj

C. Adverbs modify other adverbs.

She sang quite beautifully.
         adv   adv

He ran too fast.
      adv adv

Examples: too, very, somewhat, rather, so

6. **PREPOSITIONS**—used to show relationships of one thing to another.

Three types:

    A. Spatial (space) relationships—to, at, around, on, over, between, etc.

    B. Time relationships—after, before, during, since, until

    C. Other relationships—of, for, about, with, without, but, except, like

Prepositional phrases always begin with a preposition and end with a noun or pronoun, though they may have adjectives in the middle:

around the corner
after that big dinner
about me

Note: The subject of a sentence is never in the prepositional phrase.

7. **ARTICLES**—a, an, the

8. **CONJUNCTIONS**—used to join two sentences (also called two independent clauses) or to join parts within a sentence.

Memorize these! Everything about run-ons and fragments will be easier if you do.

and	as if	while
but	as though	so
for	as soon as	so as
or	whether	so that
nor	although	that
if	though	unless
	even though	because

Some question words, when not used in questions are conjunctions:

when	+	ever
where	+	ever
who	+	ever
what	+	ever
how	+	ever

Some common prepositions of time are also used as conjunctions:

after

before

since

It's important to know which words are **NOT** conjunctions, although many people mistake them to be. Because these are not conjunctions, they **cannot** be used to join two sentences:

however (meaning, "but")

therefore

thus

nevertheless

then

plus

SECTION XIX.

CORRECTION SYMBOLS

These correction symbols are in common usage among most English teachers. Sections treating specific mistakes are at the right.

Symbol	Meaning	Section
⋀#	insert a space	
◡	bring together; do not leave a space	
∾	transpose; reverse the order	
ℓ.c.	use lower case; don't use a capital (slash through letter)	
≡	use upper case; use a capital (3 lines under letter)	
|P|	lack of parallel construction	XVII, Part 4
# or #	new paragraph	
⊂	no new paragraph	
ℓ	take out; omit	
◯	spelling error	
sp	spelling error	
Apo	apostrophe error	XII
R-O	run-on sentence; separate into 2 sent.	XVI
frag	sentence fragment; incomplete sentence	XV
SS	error in sentence structure	
Agr	lack of agreement, subject/verb	XIV
Pro Agr	lack of agreement, pronoun/antecedent	XIV
Awk	awkward wording	
p	punctuation error	XIII
T	inconsistency in tense	
Pro	error in pronoun usage	XVII, Part 1
Rep	repetitious	VIII
Red	redundant	VIII

In addition, these abbreviations are occasionally used on student papers if this book is used in a course. Appropriate explanatory sections are indicated in the right column.

ANA GAP	Analytic Gap	II, p. 10-11; VI, p. 26-27
ATQD	Attack the question directly.	
BMS	Be more specific.	IX, #10
DM	Dangling Modifier	XVII, #4
DS	Diction Shift	IX, #14
FQ	Floating Quote	VI, p. 26-28
GP	Good Point	
GWC	Good Word Choice	
No TS	Not a proper topic sentence	
OS	Overlapping Sentences	VIII, #8
PWC	Poor Word Choice	
Tig	Tighten	VIII
WW	Wrong Word, misused word	
WO	Word order is misleading or awkward.	
Wr-O	Write out. Do not use numerals or abbreviate.	

LITERATURE-BASED ESSAY FORMAT

I. Introduction   (usually one paragraph)

   A. General comment or observation.   (Not so broad that it's obvious)

   B. Narrowing to specific topic of this paper.   (Sometimes A & B are combined into one sentence.)

   C. Title and author of work.   (Not a sentence by itself but inserted into a sentence containing other material.)

   D. Background information IF relevant.   (time period, setting, social concerns, issue, etc.)

   E. Thesis, the claim of your argument.   (see p. 5-6) Usually a one-sentence answer to the question. It should be more than a list of subtopics or a restatement of the question.

   F. Direction of support. Often a list of subtopics or subdivisions of thesis. (The number of subdivisions should be determined by the scope and complexity of question; it's not necessarily always three.)

   1.

   2.

   3.

II. First paragraph of body:

   A. Topic sentence referring to first subdivision. (More than a restatement of subtopic from I. F.)

   B. Analysis, extension, or development of first subtopic. (Discussion in abstract, without reference to specifics of plot; not a quotation.)

   C. Supporting evidence. Could be:

      1. Plot event (not the whole plot of the entire work)

      2. Item related to a character

      3. Reference to imagery, symbolism or allusion

      4. Quotation (with speaker, occasion & interpretation)

      5. Paraphrase (with speaker, occasion & interpretation)

      6. Combination of 1-5

   D. Re-anchor or return to topic sentence and/or thesis

Repeat the same pattern outlined in II for all paragraphs of body

III. Conclusion: Restatement of thesis only stronger, deeper, more insightful, with reference to subpoints, and without introducing any new topics.

SECTION XXI.

SAMPLE ESSAY

Four stages of preparing a final essay are given in this section so you can see that a substantial, polished piece of writing does not happen in one sitting. In fact, between these four samples, there may be numerous separate steps. Mechanical and structural errors appear in early drafts that are corrected later.

Here is the Essay Question:

Using an American novel, take a stance on whether the author upholds existing social conventions and attitudes or wishes to modify those attitudes and advocate social change.

A student's preliminary exploration of the question might be done as a cluster, like this:

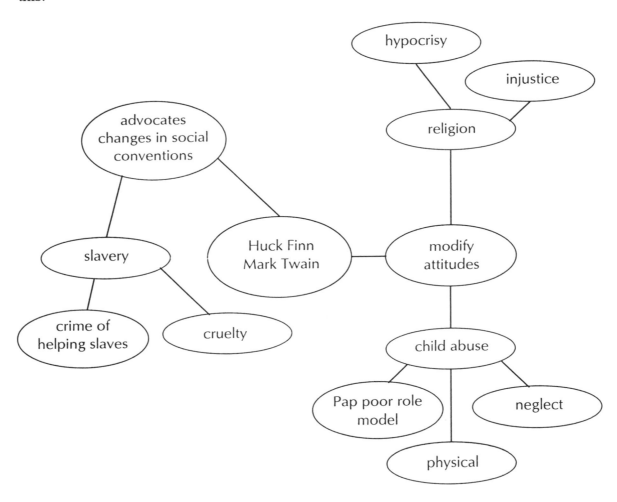

FIRST DRAFT:

Mark Twain Stars as The Advocator

In Mark Twain's <u>The Adventures of Huckleberry Finn</u>, Huck, the main character, grows up in a difficult period of time when slavery was a major issue between the North and the South. Living in the South during the time of slavery, Huck was exposed to it's injustices frequently. Twain advocates changes in social conventions from the beginning when Huck decides to help a Negro slave named Jim to freedom. This decision made by Huck clearly shows Twain wishes to modify the attitudes of people because during the times of slavery it was considered a crime to help a slave.

Helping Jim to freedom was a brave decision, even though Huck did not realize the risk. Huck did not set out to help a slave, he faked his death and ran away, and then encountered Jim. Since Jim was also running away, Huck decided to help him. On their adventure down the Mississippi River, Huck had to hide and protect Jim numerous times from men who were looking for him.

Huck did this because he did not want to lose Jim as a friend or a traveling buddy. Huck was ignorant, as many people probably were during the time of slavery, and were not well aware how cruel and inhumane slavery was. Twain once again implants the cruelty of slavery into the reader so people can see how wrong it is and hopefully end it forever.

Huck is a troubled boy growing up in a difficult time period and instead of dealing with his problems his solution is to run away from them. Huck runs away for many reasons, but the main reason was his relationship with his father. When Huck was reunited with his father, Pap, he is once again abused, both physically and mentally. After Huck observes his father's behavior, he realizes Pap is an individual who is looked down upon by society and is a poor role model for him. Huck, no longer able to tolerate the abuse, decides to run away. This is another attitude Twain wishes to modify, child abuse. Many people do not realize the devastating affects child abuse has on a person. Childhood is suppose to be the happiest time of a person's life and child abuse not only ruins the persons childhood but can also ruin the rest of their life. That is why Twain creates abusive characters such as Pap, so people can be exposed to the problems.

Twain also seems to want to change the way people think about religion. In the beginning of the novel, Huck states:

> After supper she got out her book and learned me about Moses and the Bulrushers, and I was in a sweat to find out all about him; but my and by she let it out that Moses had been dead a considerable long time; so then I didn't care no more about him because I don't stake no stock in dead people.

Throughout the novel, Huck makes these remarks that insinuate religion is unimportant and he never wants to go to church. Since Huck is essentially Twain as a child, Huck is the one expressing Twain's views. These recurring sarcastic comments about religion constantly remind the reader of Twain's view on religion.

Twain throughout the whole novel imbeds his views on society into the reader, causing the reader to think strongly on what has been read. This is exactly what Twain intended, that people will realize the mistakes that are being made and will try to overcome them, thus advocating changes in social conventions, Twain's main goal.

SECOND DRAFT:

Revision submitted by student without prior teacher evaluation.

Mark Twain: The Advocator

Throughout history, authors have commented in their books on the attitudes in society. One such author is Mark Twain. In his novel, <u>The Adventures of Huckleberry Finn</u>, Huck, the main character, grows up in a difficult period of time when slavery was a major issue between the North and the South. Living in the South during the time of slavery, Huck was exposed to it's injustices frequently. Twain advocates changes in social conventions from the beginning when Huck decides to help a Negro slave named Jim to freedom. Twain wishes to modify people's attitudes about slavery, religion and child abuse.

During the times of slavery it was considered a crime to help a slave.Helping Jim to freedom was a brave decision, even though Huck did not realize the risk. Huck did not set out to help a slave, he faked his death and ran away, and then encountered Jim. Since Jim was also running away, Huck decided to help him. On their adventure down the Mississippi River, Huck had to hide and protect Jim numerous times from men who were looking for him. Huck did this because he did not want to lose Jim as a friend or a traveling buddy, and on the journey he learns to value Jim as a good-hearted, loyal human being who loved his own family "just as white people love theirs."

Huck was ignorant, as many people probably were during the time of slavery, and were not well aware how cruel and inhumane slavery was. Twain suggests the cruelty of slavery by the separation of Jim from his family, by Jim being hunted by slave catchers who might shoot him, and by locking him in a small cabin at Aunt Sally's. In fact, at one point in the novel, Huck says, "Human beings can be awful cruel to each other." This is so people can see how wrong it is and hopefully end it forever.

Huck is a troubled boy growing up in a difficult time period and instead of dealing with his problems his solution is to run away from them. Huck runs away for many reasons, but the main reason was his relationship with his father. When Huck was reunited with his father, Pap, he is once again abused, both physically and mentally. Pap neglects to take care of Huck or feed him or see that he goes to school. In fact, Pap locks up Huck in their cabin and once goes after him with a knife. Huck, no longer able to tolerate the abuse, decides to run away. This is another attitude Twain wishes to modify, child abuse.

Many people do not realize the devastating affects child abuse has on a person. Childhood is suppose to be the happiest time of a person's life and child abuse not only ruins the persons childhood but can also ruin the rest of their life. That is why Twain creates abusive characters such as Pap, so people can be exposed to the problems.

Twain also seems to want to change the way people think about religion. While Huck is staying with the Widow Douglas he states:

> After supper she got out her book and learned me about Moses and the Bulrushers, and I was in a sweat to find out all about him; but my and by she let it out that Moses had been dead a considerable long time; so then I didn't care no more about him because I don't stake no stock in dead people.

Throughout the novel, Huck makes remarks that insinuate religion is unimportant and he never wants to go to church. Since Huck is essentially Twain as a child, Huck is the one expressing Twain's views. Even very religious people in the novel do unjust things, like continue a feud for no reason, or hypocritical things, such as supporting slavery. These recurring sarcastic comments about religion constantly remind the reader of Twain's view on religion.

Twain throughout the whole novel gives his views on society, specifically slavery, child abuse and religion, causing the reader to think strongly on what has been read. This is exactly what Twain intended, that people will realize the mistakes that are being made and will try to overcome them, thus advocating changes in social conventions, Twain's main goal.

TEACHER-CORRECTED SECOND DRAFT:

The main problems with this essay are:

1. Thesis needs sharpening. Claim needs to have more substance rather than simply listing three subtopics. Precise social change advocated and attitudes challenged need to be given.

2. Each paragraph of body needs topic sentence directly connected to thesis.

3. Analytic gap in paragraph five needs to be corrected by insightful extension of the concept in topic sentence and rearrangement of paragraph elements.

4. Last sentence of body paragraphs needs stronger re-anchor to topic sentence or thesis.

5. Inconsistent tense needs to be corrected by use of present.

6. Floating quote in paragraph five needs interpretive commentary.

7. Generalizations, especially in the conclusion, need to be replaced with more substantial commentary. Listing the three subtopics is not precise enough. What social change is he advocating?

Mark Twain: The Advocator

Too far. Start back. Start with Twain.

Throughout history, authors have commented in their books on the attitudes in society. One such author is Mark Twain. In his novel, <u>The Adventures of Huckleberry Finn</u>, Huck, the main character, grows up in a difficult period of time when slavery was a major issue between the North and the South. Living in the South during the time of slavery, Huck was exposed to it's injustices frequently. Twain advocates changes in social conventions from the beginning when Huck decides to help a Negro slave named Jim to freedom. Twain wishes to modify people's attitudes about slavery, religion and child abuse.

Rep.
Tig.
NO APO
BMS
Identify more precisely.
Out of place in introduction.
BMS. Modify them how?
① ③ ②

During the times of slavery it was considered a crime to help a slave. Helping Jim to freedom was a brave decision, even though Huck did not realize the risk. Huck did not set out to help a slave, he faked his death and ran away, and then encountered Jim. Since Jim was also running away, Huck decided to help him. On their adventure down the Mississippi River, Huck had to hide and protect Jim numerous times from men who were looking for him. Huck did this because he did not want to lose Jim as a friend or a traveling buddy, and on the journey he learns to value Jim as a good-hearted, loyal human being who loved his own family "just as white people love theirs."

BMS
No TS
R-O
OS
Tig
DS
DS
Save incident for body.
Good specificity

Huck was ignorant, as many people probably were during the time of slavery, and were not well aware how cruel and inhumane slavery was. Twain suggests the cruelty of slavery by the separation of Jim from his family, by Jim being hunted by slave catchers who might shoot him, and by locking him in a small cabin at Aunt Sally's. In fact, at one point in the novel, Huck says, "Human beings can be awful cruel to each other." This is so people can see how wrong it is and hopefully end it forever.

T
T
good specific examples
BMS – When?
/P/
usage error

Huck is a troubled boy growing up in a difficult time period and instead of dealing with his problems his solution is to run away from them. Huck runs away for many reasons, but the main reason was his relationship with his father. When Huck was reunited with his father, Pap, he is once again abused, both physically and mentally. Pap neglects to take care of Huck or feed him or see that he goes to school. In fact, Pap locks up Huck in their cabin and once goes after him with a knife. Huck no longer able to tolerate the abuse, decides to run away. This is another attitude Twain wishes to modify, child abuse. Many people do not realize the devastating affects child abuse has on a person. Childhood is suppose to be the happiest time of a person's life and child abuse not only ruins the persons childhood but can also ruin the rest of their life. That is why Twain creates abusive characters such as Pap, so people can be exposed to the problems.

No TS
BMS Identify them
was/is
T
trite
OS
Awk
WO
Too general
Stay closer to the novel.
Apo
sp

80

Twain also seems to want to change the way people think about religion. ∧While Huck is staying with the Widow Douglas he states:

> After supper she got out her book and learned me about Moses and the Bulrushers, and I was in a sweat to find out all about him; but my and by she let it out that Moses had been dead a considerable long time; so then I didn't care no more about him because I don't stake no stock in dead people.

F Q

Throughout the novel, Huck makes remarks that insinuate religion is unimportant and he never wants to go to church. Since Huck is essentially Twain as a child, Huck is the one expressing Twain's views. Even very religious people in the novel do unjust things, like continue a feud for no reason, or hypocritical things, such as supporting slavery. These recurring *PWC* sarcastic comments about religion constantly remind the reader of Twain's view on religion.

/P/

BMS

WO

Twain/throughout the whole novel gives his views on society, specifically slavery, child abuse and religion, causing the reader to think strongly on what has been read. This is exactly what Twain intended, that people will realize the mistakes that are being made and will try to overcome them, thus advocating changes in social conventions, Twain's main goal.

Weak conclusion

Listing topics is not precise enough. State the views.

BMS. State precisely what changes Twain advocates.

generalization

FINAL DRAFT:

Resubmitted version taking into account marginal notations and teacher evaluation, above, as if they had appeared on the returned paper.

Mark Twain: Advocator of Human Rights and Decency

Although on one level Mark Twain's novel, The Adventures of Huckleberry Finn, is an adventure story of a boy on a raft, it is also a record of the social attitudes, including ignorance and hypocrisy, of the pre-Civil War South. Living during the slavery of the 1840's, Huck, the main character, is exposed to its injustices frequently. Twain advocates changes in social conventions from slavery and injustice toward blacks to freedom and acceptance, as well as advocating the modification of people's attitudes to eliminate the ignorance of child abuse and the hypocrisy in religion.

The major change Twain advocates is in the institution of slavery which he sees as unjust and inhumane. Before the Civil War, it was considered a crime to help a slave, so helping Jim to freedom is a brave decision for Huck, even though Huck does not realize the risk. Huck does not set out to help a slave. While Huck is escaping from his father, he encounters Jim escaping slavery and they go down the Mississippi River together. On the journey he learns to value Jim as a good-hearted, loyal human being who loves his own family "just as white people love theirs." Huck decides to hide and protect Jim from slave hunters numerous times because he does not want to lose Jim as a friend or a traveling companion. The good relationship that develops between a white boy and a black man is Twain's way of advocating a society in which such a friendship could be possible.

Twain exposes the general ignorance of the time. Before knowing Jim, Huck is ignorant, as many people probably were during the time of slavery, and so he isn't aware how inhumane slavery is. Twain suggests the cruelty of slavery by the separation of Jim from his family, the slave hunt for Jim, and by the act of locking him in a small cabin at Aunt Sally's. In fact, at one point in the novel, Huck says, "Human beings can be awful cruel to each other." This line exemplifies the wrong involved in slavery.

Another attitude Twain wishes to expose is the ignorance of child abuse. Neglect of children apparently went unnoticed more in the 19th Century than it does today. Huck is a troubled boy neglected by his father who doesn't take care of him or feed him or see that he goes to school. The relationship with his father is so bad that Huck runs away from him. When he is reunited with his father, Pap, he is once again abused, even physically. Pap locks up Huck in their cabin and once goes after him with a knife. Because he can't tolerate the abuse any longer, Huck decides to run away for good. Childhood, which is supposed to be the happiest time of a person's life, for Huck is a time of worrying about survival. Creating abusive characters such as Pap allows Twain to expose the ignorance of neglect and cruelty and to show by comparison that Huck's relationship with Jim is a much better one. In this way, Twain advocates more humane ways of treating each other.

Twain also seems to want to change the way people think about religion. If people pretend they are devout and do cruel things, Twain feels that is not truly pious. Even very religious people in the novel do unjust things, such as feuding for no reason, or hypocritical things, such as supporting slavery. Throughout the novel, Huck makes remarks that insinuate religion is unimportant and he never wants to go to church. Since Huck is essentially Twain as a child, Huck is the one expressing Twain's views. While Huck is staying with the Widow Douglas he states:

> After supper she got out her book and learned me about Moses and the Bulrushers, and I was in a sweat to find out all about him; but my and by she let it out that Moses had been dead a considerable long time; so then I didn't care no more about him because I don't stake no stock in dead people.

Apparently Huck doesn't feel these old stories have anything to do with what he sees in the world. These recurring critical comments about religion constantly remind the reader that Twain thinks religion is sometimes hypocritical.

Throughout the novel Twain suggests that society's faults of hypocrisy, injustice, cruelty and ignorance cause problems of slavery, child abuse and religion. Twain intended that readers realize the mistakes in people's behavior and make changes, specifically eliminating slavery and child abuse and making religion have the effect of improving human rights and decency.

Note these improvements in the final draft over the second draft:

1. Thesis is sharpened using some of the words in the essay question and giving precise noun phrases naming attitudes rather than including an event in the thesis.

2. Subtopics in the introduction are in the same order as covered in the paper.

3. Tense is consistently present for all references to the action of the novel.

4. There is greater specificity throughout the paper. This is accomplished by the use of abstract nouns which give preceise names for the actions the earlier draft narrated. Examples: cruelty, injustice, hypocrisy, ignorance, decency, human rights.

5. Topic sentences which relate directly to the thesis are supplied for each body paragraph.

6. Reanchoring to thesis never lets the reader forget the primary claim governing the paper.

7. Generalizations about child abuse unattached to the novel are replaced with comments on the specific child abuse in the novel.

8. The Analytic Gap is filled with extension of the topic given in the topic sentence and the paragraph is rearranged so the quote doesn't come immediately after the topic sentence.

9. A sentence of interpretation of that long floating quote is given.

10. Words such as *suggests, exposes*, and *apparently* exhibit more appropriate essay diction making the style more academic.

11. Title is strengthened by being more precise, and the title words are used in the conclusion.

SECTION XXII.

HOW TO TAKE NOTES

"Okay, so the teacher says to take notes. Swell. But how? I can't take down everything he says; he talks too fast. My notes are a bunch of beginnings of sentences trailing off into nothing. Besides, I wouldn't know what to take down. Easier just to listen."

This frustration is close to universal. But listening sometimes isn't enough, especially in classes which test heavily on lecture material.

As far as notetaking is concerned, students come in several varieties:

Type A: This student has no notebook and rarely a pencil. He (and he, in this section, also means she) never takes notes unless the teacher glares at him or publicly derides him, shaming him into it. When he feels so uncomfortable because everyone else who's taking notes is now staring at him, he has to ask the person next to him for pencil and paper. He needn't bother. Without a notebook, the paper will get lost before class the next day.

Type B: Type B has a notebook and pencil, but they are neatly stowed in his zippered backpack beneath his desk. Far be it from him to have to get it out. When it becomes clear there is something important to take down, he reasons that it's too much effort, that it will only be a small point, that he'll remember, or that he can afford to miss it. If deeply conscience-stricken, he'll have to scramble, too, just like Type A, but he'll probably miss it.

Type C: Little Miss (or Mr.) Goody-goody has her notes out ready to go. With over-developed zeal she (or he, mind you) tries to take down everything the teacher says, or at least everything the teacher emphasizes. There's only one problem: She attempts to take it down word for word. How thorough of her, you say? Not so. She's often no better off than Type B. In trying to take down every word, she becomes frustrated. She doesn't know how to spell Thoreau or Renaissance and she struggles with it for a split second, just enough to make her forget the rest of the sentence. Her problem is that she doesn't think. She only writes. Without thinking about what the idea means, if even for a moment, she's only reproducing words mechanically. Her notes are incomplete, even though there are pages of them. Too bad. She never learned how to evaluate.

Type D: Type D is a thinker. His (or her) notes are orderly, dated, complete. They may be scribbled, but that's not important. What's essential is there. He has a separate section in his notebook for subdivisions of the course work. He doesn't try to take down entire sentences. He abbreviates. His literature notes have common abbreviations for words used frequently, like *lit* for literature, *Rom* for Romantic Period, *sat* for satire, *ir* for irony, *im* for imagery. After the first time he writes an author's name, he uses the author's initials. Mark Twain is MT, William Shakespeare is WS, Robert Frost is RF. The Renaissance is Ren and the Middle Ages is MA. He skips introductory words the teacher says, such as "the most important factor in Puritan doctrine is." Instead his notes read, "Puri doctrine = "

Type D thinks about what is being said and writes it in a way that means something to him. That means the material isn't mechanically reproduced; instead it has passed through his intellect.

Type D selects what he takes down. He looks for clues to determine what's important. He writes something down if:

1. The teacher writes it on the board. Type D takes down more than a word or a date. He writes the significance of the date, not just the date. He writes a definition of the word on the board even if the teacher doesn't write the definition but merely says it.

2. The teacher emphasizes a point vocally by speaking louder, softer, slower or at a different pace than what preceded it.

3. The teacher gets more animated or more involved in describing or proving something.

4. The teacher says "This is important," "These are famous lines," "This is a major shift in attitude," or some such direct indication.

5. The teacher numbers items. When material is numbered, it's a good clue that it's significant. Such a series may be introduced by "there are three reasons why..." or "two factors contributed to..." or "four types of literature were popular during..." or "he criticized his society for three practices...." Material that can easily be numbered often appears on multiple choice or essay tests, so Type D gets prepared.

6. The teacher says the same idea in more than one way.

In addition, Type D asks the teacher for repetition of items missed if they fell into one of these categories. Type D goes over the previous day's notes in class before the next session begins. He asks the teacher for clarification when he doesn't understand what he took down the day before.

Type D organizes his notebook graphically, uses tabs for sections, highlights important information, uses consistent headers, keeps a running record of terms with definitions introduced in class, keeps notes on writing instruction separate from notes on literature.

It should be no surprise that Type D rarely receives "D's" on tests.

GLOSSARY OF LITERARY TERMS

ALLEGORY: A narrative (story) in either verse or prose in which abstract concepts (such as pride, greed, hope, lust, love) are represented by characters, actions and elements of setting which convey a strong religious, social or political message. A well known early example is the medieval play *Everyman*.

ALLITERATION: The repetition of sounds, usually in a line of poetry, to convey mood. Assonance is the repetition of vowel sounds; consonance is the repetition of consonant sounds. Alliteration is common in Anglo-Saxon poetry such as *Beowulf* and in Edgar Allen Poe's work.

ALLUSION: A subtle reference in a work of literature to another work of literature, a historical figure or a work of art. For example, Faulkner's novel title, *The Sound and the Fury*, is taken from *Macbeth*. Shakespeare's line actually reads, "'Tis a tale told by an idiot full of sound and fury, signifying nothing." Note that the allusion is slightly different so it is not a quote. Therefore, no indication of source is needed. Many allusions come from the Bible and Greek and Roman mythology.

ANALOGY: A comparison made between two items, situations, or ideas that are alike in most or in some respects. For example, the creation of a sculpture may be likened to the building of a house. A multi-ethnic society is likened to a salad.

ANTAGONIST: The person or force working against the main character or protagonist in a work of literature.

ANTITHESIS: The juxtaposition (placing together) of contrasting ideas, as in, "A man should be mourned at his birth, not his death." Often this contrast is presented using parallel structure, as in Neil Armstrong's famous words as he stepped on the moon: "That's one small step for a man, one giant leap for mankind." Sometimes the contrasts occur in a series, as in Samuel Johnson's sentence: "Though studious, he was popular; though argumentative, he was modest; though inflexible, he was candid." This style of sentence is highly useful in setting up the thesis for an essay.

APOSTROPHE: A figure of speech in which an absent person (usually dead) or a god is addressed directly, as if the work of literature were written to or about him. (i.e. "Milton! thou shouldst be living at this hour.") Also, an emotion, state of nature or season can be addressed.

BALLAD: A narrative tale told in verse, never written but passed along in the oral tradition and often sung. Because ballads were memorized, they made use of repetition and strong rhythm and rhyme. Because they appealed to commoners, they use highly emotional events, sometimes violence and often romance. Plot is paramount; motivations and character development are rarely given.

BARD: The major poet of an entire culture; Shakespeare.

BLANK VERSE: Unrhymed iambic pentameter (five accented syllables each preceded by an unaccented syllable).

CAESURA: A definite pause near the half way point in a line of verse.

CATHARSIS: The emotional relief or cleansing that occurs after profound tragedy; the feeling of an audience—after witnessing tremendous human endurance and/or the pity of wasted greatness—that, after all, man is capable of great heights.

CLICHE: An expression or phrase so common and overused that it has become trite and meaningless. (See Section X.)

CONCEIT: An elaborate and unusual figure of speech comparing two very dissimilar things. The comparison usually extends over several lines, and may be used throughout the piece of literature.

CONNOTATION: The emotional associations connected with a word, but not the definition (which is its denotation). The connotations for the word "serpent," for example, are generally negative and involve the aspects of slyness, fear, ugliness, sting, danger, poison, temptation, evil, sin, Adam and Eve, and even the fall of man.

COUPLET: A pair of rhyming lines with identical meter.

DENOUEMENT: The resolution or settling of the plot after the climax.

DICTION: The author's choice of words or phrases. The same idea can be expressed in formal diction ("Would you be so kind, sir, as to close the door?") or informal ("Shut the door!"). Diction includes vocabulary (lexical choice) and syntax (sentence structure).

DRAMATIC IRONY: The situation in which the audience or reader is made aware of something that a character does not know.

ELEGY: A solemn, reflective poem, usually about death in general or about the death of an individual, formal in tone.

ELLIPSIS: Omission of a word or words readily implied by the context, for the purposes of brevity, smoothness or subtlety. In "Everybody's friend is nobody's," the final repetition of the word friend is understood.

EPIC: A long narrative tale, generally told in verse with a high, lofty style, involving the adventures and often the journey (either physical or spiritual) of a hero important to his culture. Upon his fate depends the welfare of his entire culture. Usually the magnitude of the tale necessitates imploring the aid of some muse in the telling of it. The setting is vast in scope, covering great nations and is often international. Supernatural forces (gods and angels) interest themselves in the action. Examples: *The Iliad, The Odyssey, Paradise Lost, Beowulf.*

FIGURATIVE LANGUAGE: Language used in a nonliteral way to create a sensual image, a pictorial effect, or freshness of expression. Figures of speech such as personification, simile, metaphor, synecdoche, apostrophe, hyperbole, oxymoron are all types of figurative language, and are divided between tropes which alter or play with meaning, and schemes which alter word order or involve repeated or eliminated elements. See entry on each term for specifics.

FOIL: A character which has a similar situation or nature than another character but with some significant differences, used as a contrast so that each may be seen more clearly by the comparison. Hamlet and Laertes in *Hamlet* are examples.

HAMARTIA: The great human error, flaw or frailty by means of which a tragic hero falls. It may be bad judgment or inherited weakness or a tendency to exhibit some specific and negative character trait.

HYPERBOLE: Intentional exaggeration for effect. ("I'll kill him if he does that again.")

IMAGE: A group of words that give a mental picture or a sensory representation of a literal object, a scene or an abstract idea.

IRONY: Figure of speech in which the actual intent is expressed in words which carry the opposite meaning. Irony is likely to be confused with sarcasm, but it differs from sarcasm in that it is lighter, less harsh, more indirect. Irony is at times marked by grim humor, an unemotional detachment, a tongue in cheek tone. It can be subtle or heavy handed.

KENNING: A figure of speech formed by two usually unrelated nouns combined to mean a third noun different from either of the two alone. Thus, "whale road" refers to ocean, "sky candle" refers to sun, and "water wind" refers to current.

LITOTES: Intentional understatement for an effect, usually humor or agreement on the part of the reader.

METAPHOR: A figure of speech using an implied comparison, calling something by the name of something else. Usually a metaphor gives to one object the qualities of the other. ("You are an angel to help me.")

METER: The recurrence in poetry of a rhythmic pattern.

METONYMY: Substitution of a word for another word closely related to it, such as cause for effect, or the container for the contained, as in using crown for king or queen, brass for military officers. "The pen is mightier than the sword." In Sir Winston Churchill's famous World War II line, "I have nothing to offer but blood, toil, tears and sweat," he was referring to the abstractions of sacrifice, commitment, passion, and hard work.

MOCK EPIC: A narrative using the lofty language, literary devices and grand sweep of an epic, but for a subject matter which intentionally doesn't merit the grandeur, done for the purposes of satire, parody or humor.

MUSE: Any of the nine sister goddesses from Greek culture who preside over poetry and song; a supernatural being said to assist storytellers in the telling of their tales.

ONOMATOPOEIA: Words in which the sound of the word imitates the sound of the thing spoken of.

OXYMORON: A figure of speech using apparent contradiction, impossibility, or paradox. The effect is produced by the seeming self-contradiction.

PARABLE: A brief fictional work which illustrates a moral or teaches a religious lesson. It differs from an allegory because the characters do not necessarily represent abstract qualities.

PARADOX: A statement or proposition which at face value is self-contradictory or absurd, yet does, nevertheless, express a truth.

PARALLELISM: Similarity of structure in a pair of phrases or clauses, or in a series of related words. The Declaration of Independence states, "We mutually pledge to each other our Lives, our Fortunes, and our sacred Honor."

PARODY: A composition burlesquing or imitating another more serious work of literature. It is designed to ridicule or criticize indirectly the original work of literature.

PERSONA: The creation by an author of a fictional person other than himself who tells the story, usually in first person. Huck Finn is a persona created by Mark Twain. The speaker in "A Modest Proposal" is not Jonathan Swift, but a persona.

PERSONIFICATION: A figure of speech which gives human form, character, attributes or sensibilities to animals, ideas, abstractions and inanimate objects.

SATIRE: The criticism or exposure of human folly, human evil or human institutions through use of irony, ridicule, shock or humor for purposes of human improvement and reform. Two forms of satire are Horatian, a lighter style which aims to correct by gentle laughter; and Juvenalian, much more harsh and bitter, a vehement outburst of contempt and moral indignation at the corruption and evil of humanity.

SIMILE: A figure of speech which describes something by comparing it to a dissimilar object using "like" or "as." The first object is described more clearly by virtue of the shared qualities of the two things.

SOLILOQUY: A speech given by a character on a stage which is understood to represent his thought process. As a convention, if there is someone else on stage, the audience understands that the other character does not hear the speaker's words.

SONNET: A 14-line poem using iambic pentameter which states a theme, a concern or an issue, and then responds to or comments on it, and sometimes resolves it. In the Italian or Petrarchan sonnet, the issue is stated in eight lines and the comment in six; in the English or Shakespearean sonnet, the issue is stated in 12 lines (three quatrains) and the comment in a couplet (two lines.)

STREAM OF CONSCIOUSNESS: The recording or re-creation of a character's flow of thought written in very informal style. It often involves intentional non-grammatical writing, sentence fragments, and a string of images.

SYMBOL: An object, word, action or event which stands for or suggests some abstraction beyond itself.

SYNAESTHESIA: The mixing of the senses in imagery; the description of an object by a sense other than the most obvious one. Wordsworth speaks of a "quiet sky," not a dark sky. In describing a jeweled necklace just removed from someone's neck, Keats doesn't describe its sparkle or shape, but the feel to the touch in his phrase, "the warmed jewels."

SYNECDOCHE: A form of metonymy in which the mention of a part of something signifies the whole thing or an abstraction, such as "hand" meaning manual assistance. The question, "Do you have wheels?" actually means "Do you have a car?". "A thousand sails upon the sea" does not mean there aren't boats under those sails.

SYNTAX: The relationship of words in a sentence or phrase which is generally held to be appropriate, conventional or correct. A syntax error is one in which the combination of words is unconventional or incorrect.

TONE: The feeling generated by a piece of literature and conveyed or produced by its diction and imagery.

INDEX